THE ART OF
ADOPTION

THE ART OF ADOPTION

Linda Cannon Burgess

W · W · NORTON & COMPANY

New York · London

Copyright © 1981, 1976 by Linda Cannon Burgess
Published simultaneously in Canada by George J. McLeod Limited, Toronto.
Printed in the United States of America

First published as a Norton paperback 1981
by arrangement with Acropolis Books

Library of Congress Cataloging in Publication Data
Burgess, Linda Cannon.
  The art of adoption.

  Includes index.
  1. Adoption—United States. I. Title.
HV881.B86 1981   362.7′34′0973   80–20847

W. W. Norton & Company, Inc. 500 Fifth Avenue, New York, N.Y. 10110
W. W. Norton & Company Ltd. 25 New Street Square, London EC4A 3NT

2 3 4 5 6 7 8 9 0

ISBN 0-393-00036-2

DEDICATION

*To my clients who in anguish,
disappointment and joy
shared their lives with me
and enriched my own
beyond all measure.*

TABLE
OF
CONTENTS

PREFACE

This book is written for all persons interested in adoption but especially for the adopted themselves and for their parents, both the birth parents and the adopters. Their lives are inexorably bound to one another but they live in different worlds of perception. Caught in the emotional web surrounding adoption, the adoptees, their birth parents and their adoptive parents are each largely ignorant of the feelings of the others. Unable to understand, they often conjure up distorted pictures warped by suspicion, envy and fear. I trust that this book will help to clarify the hidden sensibilities of each participant in the unique institution of adoption.

I was first introduced to adoption as a young student in Boston. I was impressed with the advanced ages of the workers in the adoption agencies there. They were mature and experienced, but also, after long service, traditional and, to my young mind, stuffy. As I observed their tight little world I knew quite definitely that adoption was one field of social work I would never enter. Years later when I became an adoption worker myself I understood the fascination and vitality that held those "elderly" women in its grip.

Shunning adoption I chose medical social work as my specialty and had my first job in The Children's Hospital in Boston. Little did I know how greatly this exposure to the medical problems of infants and children would contribute to my usefulness in adoption work twenty years later. My early professional life was brief, terminating after a year with the arrival of my first child. My living experience, so valuable to adoption work, had begun in earnest. With the arrival of four more children, professional work was forgotten, memories of it only infrequently recalled. So caught up was I in my daily labors, I did not yearn to resume work outside my home. Some days were routine and dull, some creative and fun, some enlightening, and each day was my very own.

These were years of maturing wisdom. How much more I learned than I taught! Yet, when I applied for a job years later, I approached the interview with trepidation. What did I know about social work? What could I say I had been doing for seventeen years? Washing diapers, pinafores and blue jeans, blowing noses and wiping away tears, reading *Doctor Doolittle* and tutoring in algebra, accompanying children to school plays, to concerts and to the Zoo, to dentists, doctors and piano teachers, walking miles through streams and up mountains, through museums and foreign lands? How could I claim any usefulness in professional work based on my alien activity of recent years?

An open-minded mental health clinic in North Shore Chicago to which I had applied took the chance. There I learned anew the technique of interviewing and recording, the application of objectivity and analysis, the use of assessment and planning. But judgment, the most crucial and indispensible attribute of the social worker, I already knew something about. Every day for years I had been making choices, sorting out the elements of my children's complicated lives, picking out the essentials from the myriad options, and visualizing the outcome of the actions they took. In the following years, as a medical social worker in The Evanston Hospital in Illinois, I witnessed the heartbreaking separation of unmarried mothers from their newborn infants as their babies were removed by the adoption workers of The Cradle Society. I was especially struck by the timing of the separation, which occurred two or three days after delivery when the mother's instinctive protectiveness of her infant was at its peak. It seemed barbaric. At the same time I was witnessing grief-stricken women unable to conceive who were searching by medical means to reverse the fate of their sterility. Month after month their hopes for conception would rise only to be dashe'd over and over again. They felt inadequate as women and as wives. They yearned for children.

What a dichotomy! I was both moved and intrigued by these opposing emotional struggles. As a mother I could not imagine parting with any one of my children and, as a woman, I could not imagine a life without them. I identified with both the unmarried mother giving up her baby and with the married woman seeking hers.

I knew firsthand a lot about the way people lived in this country. I had made my home in metropolitan areas, in city suburbs, in small towns, and on rural farms from east to west across the United States. I was as comfortable with a taciturn laborer as with a discursive intellectual. I was not overawed by persons of wealth or prominence.

I had studied psychology and was aware of the effects of childhood experience on adult behavior. I also knew from personal experience the depths to which the human spirit may be plunged, yet revive with hope and optimism. I gained perspective on myself during two years of psycho-therapy. My suffering strengthened rather than defeated me, and from the longer viewpoint of my years of living, I could transmit the force of my optimism to those whose lives I touched in their moments of intense sorrow. I knew that my life's experiences had prepared me well for work in adoption.

And so I began as a case worker in a small adoption agency in Washington, D.C. which employed only one worker besides myself. Thus I had the opportunity of learning about all the branches of adoption which in larger agencies were separately handled by different staff members. From the director of the agency, who was a lawyer, I received invaluable lessons in the law. I was given a free hand in counseling unmarried mothers, interviewing adoptive applicants, and directing the overall functions of the agency.

In the following 20 years of adoption work, I participated in approximately 900 adoptions, a tiny fraction of the total number in the United States. Yet with each one I wondered how the children had fared after the final adoption separated them from me and from the adoption agencies where I had known them. Driven by my eagerness to learn what adoption had meant to the children, what questions had been asked and how their parents had handled adoption with them, I revisited 45 homes where children I had placed since 1954 were growing up. The 146 adoptees I refound ranged in age from two to 22.

It occurred to me that adopters fearing investigation might refuse to talk to me. But I found on the contrary that the special relationship that had once linked us in the gift of life now enhanced our renewed acquaintances. The openness of the parents and their desire to help were impressive and universal. Not one adopter refused to see me.

During my years of counseling birth mothers and fathers there were great changes in the moral climate in the United States. In the earlier period I would frequently encounter the run-away pregnant girl who refused to reveal her condition to her family and gave up her baby in shame; later the teenage couple affectionately holding hands as they asked that their baby be adopted since they were not ready for marriage; and finally the liberated young woman who wished to discuss in cool logic the merits of adoption as compared with abortion.

My knowledge of grown adoptees comes from men and women in their thirties and older who have actively engaged in search of their origins. I have participated as witness in several court hearings in New York in which adult adoptees have petitioned for the opening of their sealed records.

Most adoptive parents are puzzled and alone in dealing with questions of adoption as they arise. They receive little help from other parents or from social workers, psychologists or psychiatrists, the majority of whom still acknowledge no intrinsic problems in the adoption situation. From the early reassurance that the adopted baby is the same as if born to them, the parents slowly recognize the added dimension that the status of adoption creates. For implicit in adoption are some undeniable facts: birth by another, illegitimacy, secretiveness, mystery, social stigma and genetic amputation.

Can these elements in adoption be ignored? I think not. For adoption raises conflicts of identity and loyalty in adopted individuals and, for their adopters, a unique challenge to parenthood.

Since the mid-sixties, when the agencies could scarcely handle all the adoptions they were asked to arrange, there has been a steady decline in the number of babies available for adoption. But even as adoption recedes it remains a subject of deep interest to millions of Americans of several generations. The number of individuals already adopted is tremendous, five million in the United States alone. According to these statistics from The Children's Bureau of the Department of Health, Education and Welfare, half the adoptees are under the age of eighteen. As the peak of the adoptive placements occurred in the mid-sixties, an overwhelming number of adoptees are now moving into the difficult period of their adolescence.

All the cases I have related in this book are true though I have changed names and made some attempts to disguise identities. Except for the recent interviews I have written entirely from memory. If adoptive parents, birth parents, grandparents or children think they recognize themselves, they probably do. On the other hand there is something so universal in human experience that individuals, identifying with the stories, may think mistakenly that I have written about them.

I trust my account will prove interesting to all readers and helpful to those about whom I have written. If the adopted and their parents find this book enlightening and reassuring, they should be aware that it is they, themselves, who speak to each other through me.

Linda C. Burgess
February, 1977

1 THE SOCIAL WORKER AND THE AGENCY

"MY WIFE AND I WANT TO ADOPT a baby. But I must tell you right away our circumstances. We do not want to come to see you only to be turned down. We have already been turned down by three agencies, one of them even after being accepted for a meeting of adoptive applicants."

Listening at the receiving end of this phone call, I was skeptical. Any couple turned down by three agencies, especially during a peak time when adopters were needed, must really be impossible. But I asked, "What are the circumstances?"

Mr. Brown, the applicant, explained that he had an invalid daughter at home who they expected might be institutionalized within a year. Two brothers had preceded her into institutional care at the ages of six and seven. All three children had been stricken with a rare affliction of genetic origin which gradually reduced the young children, both physically and mentally, to utter helplessness. They wanted to be a family with children and they would have no more of their own. Mr. Brown was sure he and his wife would be good parents for an adopted child. He pleaded to be seen. He hoped an interview could be arranged right away.

"When our eldest son was first sick," he said, "and nobody could diagnose the illness, we remained busy and comforted by our healthy second son. When the diagnosis was made and its genetic character was explained, we were fearful for our healthy son, but were reassured by the doctors that the chances of his also inheriting the affliction were one in thousands. We still wanted two children so that after our first-born was permanently hospitalized, we brought our daughter into the world. We lived a normal family life for one year. Then our second son showed signs of the disease. During his illness, as with our other boy, we still had one more—our daughter. She brought joy and hope to us in the midst of our sorrow. Our second son's deterioration was quicker and he was hospitalized at the age of six."

"We were again assured by our doctors that our daughter would not be afflicted. They assumed the little known disease was sex-linked and would not affect a girl. When we began to notice our daughter's stumbling walk and her incoherent speech, we knew the heavy hand of fate was descending again."

"Our doctor speculated that our apprehension might be causing her behavior, and we hoped in our hearts that they were right. We entered sessions of psychological therapy, but the deterioration of our daughter overtook the study of ourselves and raced on. She is now in a wheelchair, and she can no longer speak, but she knows us still, and we will keep her with us until she can no longer recognize us. This time, it is harder than before. We have no young growing child with whom we can build a normal life. It is hard to be positive and look forward, when there is nothing ahead." Stunned and overwhelmed, I managed to ask, "Did the other agencies tell you why they turned you down?"

"Oh yes," he explained. "They said we would have to come to terms with our daughter's death before we would be ready for adoption. They feared we would be merely replacing her with an adopted child, that we would be over-protective and apprehensive in the light of our experience. They wanted us to adjust to a life without children before we applied to adopt. They suggested that we might return two years after our daughter was institutionalized."

In what must have seemed hours of silence to Mr. Brown, I groped for an answer as my thoughts raced in many directions. Suppose we accepted their application, gave them hope and then felt compelled to turn them down. Could I add this rejection to their sorrow? Suppose we denied them even the chance to be heard. Was that fair? Should I fall back on an agency policy—against placing infants in a home where another child is sick—and let myself out of the dilemma that way? I could always use the social agency's old cliché, "We are understaffed and over-extended and couldn't possibly get to your case for months." I understood what the other agencies had been thinking, all sound considerations, but I was not convinced that this situation could be judged or dismissed in a phone interview. I thought how arbitrary we social workers are in analyzing situations superficially, in generalizing and putting clients into categories, in making hasty judgments on the basis of professional doctrine.

I concluded the other agencies were playing safe. This case presented countless problem areas to be explored, with slim chance that the Browns could have endured their tragedy without permanent personal damage. Could the Browns, after all they had suffered, provide a wholesome home for an adopted child? With the outcome so doubtful, was an investigation worth the slim chance of success? But I could not justify a rejection without seeing and talking with them.

Breaking the long pause, I said, "Yes I will see you. But please don't count on too much. Unlike our usual procedure, I'll come to your home and see the three of you together as a beginning." I made an appointment for the following week.

I'll never forget the visit, so vividly is it etched in my mind: the shrunken little girl in the pink party dress, too big around for her thin body, the large questioning eyes, the babbling speech, the long thin legs no longer able to hold her up; her father, strong and disciplined, tenderly carrying her out to the garden or up to her bed; her mother, patient and loving, filling her daughter's days with the games, the books, the joys of each age as she passed backward into infancy. I tried to remain professionally objective. Sympathy expressed in the face of such tragedy would have been trite.

The Browns had retained the will to live fully, positively, and with delight in their existence. I came away, knowing that I had seen two of the most spirited, loving, kind, courageous, and broken-hearted human beings that I would ever behold.

The rest of the adoption study took all the self-discipline and analytical powers I could muster. Burying my compassion, I questioned their anxieties, sense of guilt, motivations, loss, desire merely to replace their children. I investigated their reactions to crises and sickness, their stability, their marriage, their social life, their finances, their plans, their health, and their work. Moving into the adoption area, I explored their feelings about illegitimacy, raising adopted children, and attitudes toward birth parents.

Open, intelligent, spirited, and realistic, strongly motivated to life with adopted children, the Browns showed me how frail are the surmises we social workers can make.

Two months later a healthy boy was placed in the Brown's home. As he grew in strength, his sister weakened. Within six months, she joined her older brothers in the institution. Mrs. Brown, selfless and positive to the end, gave thanks that her daughter had

had a few months to know her little brother, though neither one would ever remember the other.

-- -- -- -- -- -- -- -- -- --

Adoptions in the United States increased steadily, peaking in the 1960's. Two factors made adoption appealing. Legislation was enacted in one state after another giving adoptive parents both protection and full parental authority. Simultaneously the study of psychology emphasized environment rather than heredity as a more important factor in child development. Parents saw the chance, through the environmental influence of their homes, to erase in their adopted children the hereditary components which, it was assumed, were of dubious quality. In the new thinking, the personality and character of their adopted children could be molded and the children would be as if born to them.

Social workers, responding to the innovative psychology of Freud, became environmentalists. Knowledge of Freud's teachings sharpened insights and greatly enhanced their understanding of people. They had found a hitching post in the amorphous science of human behavior.

The study of child psychology gave increasing evidence of the importance of the first months of life in the development of personality. This resulted in earlier placement of babies for adoption. Instead of being held in foster homes for months, to assure their mental and physical perfection for adoption, infants were placed in adoptive homes within weeks after birth.

Each adoption begins with the appearance of the expectant mother. She is usually unmarried, terrified and ashamed. She possesses limited resources and no place to hide from public view. She often requires assistance in finding lodgings, financial support and medical care. These are the first practical problems to work on. A more prolonged but equally critical effort for the social worker is to give the mother courage and reassurance and to counsel her in the ultimate decision she must make for her baby.

The expectant mother has several options open to her in dealing with her situation. During the later months of her pregnancy she might remain protected in her family home or choose to live independently in an apartment of her own. Through the assistance of social service agencies, she might live in a maternity home with other pregnant women like herself, or in a private "wage home" where she could board and earn money for her medical care.

During the last two or three months before her delivery, the social worker usually sees the expectant mother at least once a week and more often if emergencies arise. In my practice I gave mothers my home phone number a few weeks before they were to deliver. Usually the first news of the birth came from the mother herself who, still benumbed by the effects of anesthesia, would phone me to share with muffled voice the great event. Often I was her only friend as the secret of her out-of-wedlock pregnancy was known only to me.

The adoption worker is an outsider in the hospital. She must yield to the authority of the doctors, nurses, and hospital administration. Sometimes there is conflict when what the social worker considers to be in the patient's best interest is not what the institution regards as orderly procedure. I remember once rescuing a two-month-old baby boy from a hospital where he was a participant in a psychological research project. The research consisted of studying the effects on the development of babies as a result of their being held several hours a day by high school volunteers. Those in the control group were held only for feeding. I met resistance in my attempt to take him "out of research" even though I had with me the relinquishment for adoption signed by his mother. Finally I had to go to the administrator of the hospital before I could take him to a real home where he could be held forever by real parents.

On the day the mother is discharged from the hospital, her baby is taken to a temporary foster home. A mother might accompany the worker to see where her baby would be cared for, but usually the social worker transports the three-day-old infants by herself. I used to strap the well-wrapped bundles in the seat-belt by my side. A baby basket with lace and ribbons might have made a prettier picture, but I found my method was simpler and safer.

The period in the foster home gives the agency worker an ideal chance to observe the baby's progress and allows the mother time to make decisions and plans for her child. The agencies where I worked provided the foster and medical care for the babies but not for the mothers whom we felt should be under no obligation to surrender their children because of financial support we had extended them. The agency provided no permanent foster care so a mother had to decide within a few weeks whether to keep or relinquish her baby for adoption. In certain instances this period of time might be extended or the baby could be transferred for long-term foster care to another agency. I was convinced that an infant should have the love of a permanent mother as soon as possible, either the one who had given birth or an adopting one. For the baby's sake I urged decision. Very rarely did a change in the mother's circumstances alter her original plan. But her emotions often did.

Once the mother signs a relinquishment of parental rights and the biological father consents to adoption, the agency moves for an immediate placement of the baby in adoption. In the District of Columbia the papers of consent, together with the background material on the baby and his new parents, are then submitted to the court where the judge reviews the findings. In Washington no personal appearance in court is required. Through an interlocutory decree adopting parents may take their baby as soon as the adoption papers are filed. The adoption becomes final automatically at the end of six months unless set aside for good cause, the burden of proof resting with the agency. In some cases, notably with independent adoptions, the petition to adopt is initiated six months to a year after the child is placed. If there is any question about the parent-child adjustment, as with the adoption of an older child, the latter plan allows for easier removal of the adoptee.

In most agencies, a separate division of social workers is assigned solely for counseling birth mothers, those who keep their babies as well as those who surrender them for adoption. For these young clients, the social worker must be both a sensitive friend with practical insight and a wise compassionate mother. Would that all of us possessed these qualities.

Counseling is most effective over a period of several months before the birth of the child. Counseling is not brain washing. A conscientious social worker encourages the exploration of all possible avenues for keeping a baby as well as for surrendering him, even if adoption is the decision her client thinks she has already made.

By dwelling on the psychological causes of out-of-wedlock pregnancies, social workers have tended to ignore the basic cause of impregnation—sex. Psychologically speaking, an unmarried mother drawn to her seductive father may have been unconsciously running from these emotions to a relationship with a peer; but, she may also have been carried away in normal sexual passion. Ten years ago, the stated aim of counseling was to prevent further pregnancies by uncovering the unconscious motivations causing them. Counseling in contraceptive techniques was not considered a solution.

The claim has often been made by social work professionals that their counseling of pregnant unmarried mothers had brought about remarkable changes in the maturity and insight of their clients. In my experience, the awakened comprehension and the spiritual growth in mothers (those in their late teens and older) had little to do with counseling: it was their suffering, their anguish, their tie with creation, their mothering which carried them into another dimension of life. This precipitous growth was seldom seen in young teenage mothers who, still self-centered and immature, were emotionally unready to experience motherhood in depth.

The examination and appraisal of adoptive applicants is a demanding task and requires rapid assessment by the adoption worker. Only with long experience and a clear sense of her own values can she handle this sensitive and vital area well.

In the first interview she is confronted by couples (and sometimes single applicants) whom she must analyze and evaluate as potential parents. A final judgment is usually made after only four or five interviews, conducted with prospective parents both individually and together. The total inquiry is called "home study," although the visit to the home is usually made only once. Whenever questions arose I found that prolonging the study was rarely fruitful because concern for the problems of the clients tended to hamper an objective assessment.

All adoptive applicants are nervous and scared at the prospect of an investigation of their lives. Putting them at their ease is essential if a thorough study is to be made. I found it effective to meet at first in groups. In this way adoptive parents could become acquainted with me in an informal session in which I could give them a short explanation of the way the agency worked and what they could expect. The most frequent question asked at these meetings was, How long will it take? After years of indecision it is amazing how impatient the adopters become once they have made up their minds. Usually it took from two to six months to complete a study and receive a baby in the heyday of the nineteen-sixties. After the group meetings the individual interviews commenced. The initiative for pursuing the study was always left to the clients so that the faint-hearted would be able to gracefully withdraw.

There is an art to interviewing, the most important element of which is to listen. With some clients who are shy and reserved one has to draw out the life story. With others one has to peel away the surface to get beneath self-conscious bluster. A skilled interviewer needs no set questions. However I did have one with which I usually began the first interview. "What is the reason you have no children?" I would ask. The question cut deep. The couple's reaction told me a lot about their feelings for each other and their acceptance of sterility. Their response either demonstrated an ability to be open or a reluctance to disclose information on sensitive matters. From their responses I could anticipate the reactions they might have to the discomforting questions their children might ask in future years.

With no set questions there are no set answers. Yet after interviewing hundreds of adoptive applicants I came to see certain patterns of response. When these typical reactions were absent or if some bizarre notions were introduced I took a second look. For example one client, who had never been pregnant, told me she was anticipating nursing the infant she hoped to adopt. She was trying to stimulate lactation through the sucking efforts of a friend's newborn. What was wrong? I saw a well-meaning woman but one completely off-base. In trying to realize her own needs to be a complete and lactating mother, she was frustrating the hungry baby of a friend, experimenting at his expense. She was making a ritual out of nursing with no evidence that she could be successful. But most serious for a child she might adopt, she was creating a fiction by simulating natural motherhood and waiving the reality of adoption. An adopted child raised in such an unreal and confused environment would surely be a puzzled individual if not a bewildered neurotic.

Often a picture of the adopter's ideas, values and goals was revealed in discussions of subjects far removed from adoption. I found family histories and the ways in which couples earned their livings most enlightening. I heard more about systems analyses and computer programming than I could ever really comprehend. Yet, by the time they finished telling me about their mysterious work, I found I had learned a lot about the narrators themselves.

Following the interviews and a visit to the home, reference letters from the applicant's family, friends and employers completed the home study. After a review of the findings a couple was either accepted for the placement of a child in adoption or rejected and free to apply elsewhere. About one fifth of all applicants were rejected, not, I found, for insecure motivations in wanting children but because of their own agitated and unstable personalities. When I became an agency director the final responsibility was mine. I felt that a clear decision even for those who were rejected was kinder than allowing them to linger on in false anticipation of eventual acceptance. Their resentment at being judged inadequate by strangers who had known them such a short time was understandable. I usually informed rejected applicants by letter, giving them the opportunity to grieve or rage in private. This also saved me from witnessing directly the pain I was causing.

The couples who were accepted basked in anxious anticipation of the phone call that would inform them of their babies' arrival. Within a day or two after the call, the new infant member of the family, usually two or three weeks of age, would move into their home and change their lives.

After the placement I visited the adoptive home periodically, usually three times within six months after the adoption. Even though they were made in a spirit of helpfulness, adopters were relieved when these visits ceased and the baby became legally theirs. Then, at last, they were on their own.

The general structure of the process of adoption changed little during my professional career. As the number of adoptions increased and my responsibilities as director grew, I was forced to relinquish some of my work to others. However, I reserved for myself the first interview with every adopting couple and with every birth mother and father. Thus my intuitive feeling for the appropriate placement of each child above and beyond the recorded findings was mine to apply. My decisions were final—900 in all.

Adoption workers are confronted by countless diverse situations. In choosing homes for children they are constantly weighing alternative possibilities. They are often limited in their choices and place children not in what they may consider the perfect home but the best available.

Agencies are taken to task for certain adoptions. But what should a worker do, confronted with the following choices? Should a black child be placed in the only available adoptive home which is white, or grow up in a series of foster homes which are black? Will adoption into an alien American home be more disruptive to a five-year-old boy than remaining in an Asian orphanage with his peers in his own culture? Is it better that an infant born with a serious heart defect be placed immediately with a middle-aged couple, able to handle the special care necessary, or that she remain in a medically supervised foster home for several years until the defect can be corrected? Should a permanently crippled Catholic infant be adopted by the only available parents, who are Protestant, or remain in a Catholic institution where he will retain his religion? The surface appearances and the apparent contradictions in agency standards do not tell the whole story.

The choice of parents for the babies to be adopted is usually a consensus of the adoption workers in conference. The unmarried mother's counselor may identify with her client and display strong convictions in the choice of adoptive parents for her client's child. On the other side, the adoptive family investigator may be enamored of one family over another. It is helpful when foster parents are also allowed a voice because of their intimate knowledge of the developing child.

After examining the unusual factors in each case, and after discussing and analyzing the known data about both birth parents, alternative adoptive families, and the baby himself, one lets the facts ferment. The choice ultimately becomes one of judgment as to which family will be best for the child. Given a few days, the pieces seem mysteriously to come together and the choice can then be made.

Adoption workers have little knowledge of adopted children after early childhood. The void that follows adoptive placement stunts their recognition of the adoptee as a grown person. The majority of adoption workers do not see or even sense that the children they placed pass through childhood and puberty into adulthood. Like the birth mother whose vision of her child remains fixed in infancy when she surrendered him, the adoption worker associates adopted children with their ages at placement when she last saw them.

Adoption agencies have attempted to sponsor meetings of adopters to discuss post-adoptive problems without much success. Adoptive parents eschew such meetings. They do not wish to become preoccupied with adoption and be diverted from the feelings of normal parenting. Furthermore children easily sense their parents' concerns about adoption. They resent being talked about as if they and their adoption were abnormal.

2

ADOPTING PARENTS

I REMEMBER A TENSE AND ANXIOUS couple who came to me for their first interview. The wife was English, the husband American. They had met during World War II and had married in England. The husband's bombastic arrogance, leveled at the hated "Krauts", voiced for his gentle wife the feelings she could not express. To her, he appeared the typical lively, outgoing American, who had the qualities she yearned for but did not possess.

After the war they came to the United States, to his family home in Mississippi. The contempt he had so vehemently expressed for the Germans he now leveled at the blacks. The vitriolic slander that made him feel a man made her cower in embarrassment and shame. The dissimilarity which had attracted them to each other now separated them. The gregarious American had become a vulgar show-off and the reserved Englishwoman a depressed and homesick alien.

During the interview, the wife seemed to comprehend that a child would not modify her husband's behavior or cure her loneliness. The interview forced the couple to examine their true feelings and revealed to them their lack of mutual interest, understanding and ability to communicate. They had thought their childlessness made them unhappy, but found instead that their marriage was meaningless and hollow. It was obvious that I had to reject their application. The unexpected came two days later when I received a bouquet of roses. Enclosed was a card of thanks from the wife.

— — — — — — — — —

Raising adopted children is not an ordinary task and not every couple can handle it well. So choices must be made. Subjectively speaking I sought parents who showed enthusiasm, stability, tolerance and, most of all, ability to grow. I viewed as negative characteristics tension in their relationships, rigidity, immaturity, sexual incompatibility, and indecisiveness in commitment to adoption. It is important to know what motivates couples to adopt and whether, through a child, they are attempting to alleviate insoluble personal problems.

In searching for the essence of adoptive applicants, the examination of family patterns usually yields the evidence of growth and ability to handle stressful situations from which future behavior may be projected. Couples who come from whole and happy families are considered better potential parents than are those whose parents are divorced, alcoholic or neglectful. But one cannot generalize. Many persons far from following in the footsteps of troubled parents grow up to be distinctly different. Through their childhood deprivations some learn to accept frailty and to be tolerant and forgiving. Their knowledge of hardship may have better prepared them for the problems of life than the couples raised in peace and plenty.

In past decades a good income and regular church attendance were considered essential attributes for adopting couples. I found the management of money more important than the amount. Church membership, a requirement in sectarian agencies, was not a primary consideration in non-denominational ones. I believed that adopting couples who loved life and each other enough to take a stranger's child as their own showed enough faith to be acceptable.

The family planning in yesterday's world was to have one's own children and only if that was not possible would one adopt. As adoption was a second choice, only highly motivated couples would consider it.

In my experience, if the husband was the sterile partner, he was interested in adoption primarily for his wife's sake. After the initial disbelief in his sterility, he was chagrined and spoke of being "to blame" for their childlessness. But he was more likely to come to terms with the facts than was his wife, whose more rudimentary needs remained unfulfilled.

I have sometimes witnessed the momentary withdrawal and depression of an adopting mother when she first sees her child-to-be. She is often a woman who could have borne children but for her husband's infertility. It is as if she were saying, "This could have been my own daughter. Now I will never give birth."

Most women, after adopting, are content in their adoptive motherhood. But there are some so deeply embittered by not producing their own that when their adopted daughters give birth to their own children their suppressed resentment and jealousy emerges. Today, when having children is not considered the only pattern of a woman's life, infertile women may have less sense of inferiority and unfulfillment. I found it interesting that women who had adopted children and subsequently found themselves pregnant were often upset instead of joyful, in some way feeling that they were letting down their loved adoptees.

In some families the adoption of children seemed to bring about conception and they would thus become mixed families of both adopted and birth children. The belief that once a couple adopts the wife will become pregnant is a persistent one. The occurrence is not usual (3% in my experience) but it does happen so that some adopters, holding to the expectation, adopt a girl first, in faith that a son will be born to them afterwards.

The psychological component in conception, if in fact it is not physiological, is a mysterious phenomenon. I remember a couple, tense and anxious, whom I interviewed as applicants for an infant to adopt. They had no medical problems to prevent conception. After the interview, I suggested that they seek psychiatric treatment and, if that did not work, return to me in six months. The skeptical couple, willing to do anything to have their own baby, called back three months later. The wife had conceived and they were elated, giving me all the credit. So much for an instinctive and lucky impulse.

I have known several pregnancies to occur immediately following a couple's decision to file an application for adoption, or after they had been accepted as prospective adopters. And more than once a second child was born nine months to the day after the first adopted child went home with the adopting couple. One child, whose older brother had been adopted less than a year before he was born into the family, asked his parents, "Why didn't you just wait for me?"

Social workers give great weight to the adoptive parents' readiness to adopt. A hesitant, wavering or unformed desire to adopt results in only a partial acceptance of the baby himself. Social workers learn to gauge and interpret the adopters' ambivalence, not necessarily in order to reject them, but to wait for the passage of time to strengthen their convictions.

The adoption worker's power to reject applicants can stir up resentment and even threats of reprisal. As the reasons for rejection are personal and confidential, the public as well as the clients take us to task. Testimonials on the client's behalf from friends and relatives are apt to be more loyal than perceptive. Friends of a lifetime know the applicant differently from a social investigator. Our reasons for rejection, often based on obscure deductions, can hardly ever be put into the specific language clients ask for.

It would be simpler if all rejections could be by measurable criteria such as length of marriage, age, religious affiliation, etc. These standards are often applied initially, but only in limiting the number of applicants. They become more restrictive when there are fewer babies to adopt and more liberal when more adopters are needed.

In the early days of adoption, "matching" the babies with the appropriate adoptive families was largely based on elements of physical appearance. Adoption workers were commended when children looked so much like their adopters that no one would know that they were adopted. In the 1950's adoption workers began to look beneath the surface appearances for other factors of heritage such as family traits and talents. They matched children with parents of similar backgrounds, anticipating that the adoption would develop smoothly if the biological background was like the adoptive one.

Today, matching abilities on the basis of natural heritage has acquired sinister implications, suggesting even racial bias. Every child is now considered to have equal potential. To believe otherwise implies intolerance and the undemocratic idea that all children are not created equal. According to this philosophy, some agencies ignore matching entirely and place children at random or by turn.

Putting families together in adoption is not a science. It is an art. The decisions and choices in the hands of a computer merely lining up components would leave out all the subtle elements of judgment which make certain choices appropriate and others not fitting. The art of adoption requires the analysis of factors using the head with thoughtful study and the heart with instinct. I am not sure it can be taught but I am sure its requirements are familiar to all workers charged with the task. Detrators of adoption workers say we are "playing God," but conscientious social workers, thoughtful and deliberate in coming to decisions for children's adoptions, hardly feel omnipotent. "Playing along with God" would be a more accurate description.

From the beginning to the end of the adoption study, adoption workers are constantly assessing the applicants not just as potential parents but as parents of adopted children. The openness with which applicants anticipate adoption, the sensitivity they show toward human problems and their conviction that adoption for them is a true and abiding desire are essential elements in the consideration of adoptive applicants.

No matter how well motivated and trained in rational analysis, social workers, being human, are bound to make subjective judgments. This explains why clients may be turned down in one agency and accepted in another. The pain of rejecting eager and well-intentioned adoptive applicants can be borne and justified by the social worker only in her unswerving dedication to her first responsibility and her chief client, the child. If she is torn within the adoptive triangle she may become confused and misdirected. If she is single-minded in her desire to serve the baby, she will not accept unsuitable adopters despite pressure from prominent citizens, agency doctors and board members, priests, or judges.

Some adoption workers lose their balance with the weight of authority and power their position gives them. Their domination and rigidity may cause the adopters to endure a dislocated experience and be forever haunted by the memory of their adoption study. They will be thankful only if they have succeeded in gaining a child from it. A different kind of relationship develops between the social worker and the adopters when there is consideration and respect throughout the study. Having been the vehicle through which a life was conferred, the social worker becomes a sort of omnipotent creature in the eyes of the adopters.

It is important to please adopters in the selection of their babies. For the adopters, unlike birth parents, do not have nine months of gestation to get used to, to prepare for, and to love even *in utero* the baby that is coming. Instead adopters are confronted at a moment's notice with a baby already born and awaiting their acceptance. With virtually a one-day pregnancy, an adopting couple's first view of a wrinkled two-week-old infant may either shock or delight the inexperienced adopters. It is better if they are delighted, for their first reaction may set the tone of their love of the child forever.

I considered carefully the partialities and prejudices that adoptive applicants expressed concerning the kind of children they would like to adopt. Since the sex of the child is an option the adopters have, this option must be granted. If they have secretly desired a girl and are given a boy, they do not adjust as readily to the disappointment as do birth parents, who are not, as yet, able to make a choice.

I regarded seriously even notions which seemed to me unreasonable. I found that parents who might be very pleased by and make fine parents for one child were quite unsuitable for another. On the other hand applicants who were exacting and demanding of certain qualities in the adoptees might actually be unprepared to adopt at all and unconsciously making rejection inevitable.

Color of skin, hair and eyes of babies for adoption are of great importance to many adopters. I came to regard their views with skepticism. The variations are infinite, the color often misleading as a clue to the heritage. A Greek child might have a darker complexion than a child of the Negro race. A white couple, finding the Greek child quite acceptable, would reject the lighter skinned black child as being too dark. Some parents, fearful of dark skinned Mediterranean people, asked that their children be chosen from ethnic backgrounds of northern Europe. Others were thrown by the small patch on the skin at the base of the spine, common in the Oriental race. Couples who usually saw themselves a shade lighter than they actually were, waited until they could adopt a child even two shades lighter than that. Some prospective parents could not abide curly red or kinky black hair. There were those who could accept Indian red but not Mexican brown. I concluded that not everyone had an eye for color, only an emotion that discolored the vision.

Some adopters are initially unsettled by the apparent happenstance of adoptive placements. They envision their much-loved children in other homes. They wonder what other children might have been theirs. In self-protection they cling to the belief that their children were meant to be theirs, provided through an act of God as in normal birth rather than through a choice made by a fallible human. Who can say that the maze of circumstances that leads one particular child into one certain home is not predestined? Adopters need to live with that faith and they do. Even those initially disappointed in the children selected for them accept their destiny gracefully.

3

BIRTH MOTHERS

ADELE WAS IN HER LATE TWENTIES, an unflappable, sophisticated woman, who enjoyed the freedom of her single status. When she became pregnant, she decided, like two close friends of hers, to place her expected baby in adoption. One friend had taken the independent route and used a lawyer to locate an adoptive family; the other had used the adoption agency. Adele did both.

It was most confusing. First she would see the lawyer, then come to see me. She was drawn to him because his arrangements were already made. He knew a well-to-do older couple who had been told about her and had agreed to take the baby directly from the hospital. She would not have to see it. They had agreed to pay all her expenses. The adoption through the lawyer was all set.

At the agency she found the plans tentative. Only after the baby's birth would we accept her decision for adoption as final. Only then would we alert the adopters and make arrangements for adoption. They would be chosen from a number of applicants for their suitability for her particular child. They would pay her no money for her expenses.

Adele questioned our methods as against her lawyer's. Since the agency would profit by the adoption, why shouldn't we pay her expenses? I tried to explain that a non-profit adoption agency neither makes money nor does it buy babies. I explained our thinking that she must be free of pressure and financial obligation when her baby was born. In that way her decision to keep her baby as well as to adopt would be unfettered. She saw no point in this, as she was sure she had already made her decision for adoption. Adele wished she could know about the adopting family before the baby came. She disliked delaying the baby's adoption until two weeks after he was born. The only thing she seemed to like about us was the fact that we chose adopters from a number of applicants with consideration for the baby's background and welfare.

I pressed Adele to give me the address of the baby's father so that we could obtain his consent to the adoption and information about him for the better choice of parents and for the adoption record. She understood why I wanted it but was afraid to tell me. Her lawyer had threatened her with dire consequences if she or if we contacted the alleged father. The reason for his threats became clear later. He was attempting to extort additional payment of "expenses" from the father. If the father were to know of and encourage placement through the agency instead, the lawyer would be out thousands of dollars.

Protected by his own attorney, the baby's father had remained in the background. His attorney, well versed in the ways of shysters, refused to send money except to the mother directly. This the mother's lawyer prevented by keeping his client's whereabouts unknown. The mother was unaware of these negotiations.

Adele came to see me regularly and began to express doubts about the couple her lawyer had chosen. They began to appear old and stuffy. She was now completely confused. Her lawyer could not be prosecuted for making a private adoption in the state where he practiced and the mother would not choose between us. It seemed like a lost cause to me.

One morning I received an urgent call from Adele. She was in the hospital the baby had been born, and her lawyer was on his way. When I reached her bedside the lawyer was already there. The sides were joined. The lawyer was nonplussed when I appeared and stricken by Adele's firm statement. "Everything is clear to me now. My baby is the most important person in the world. She is going to have the best chance I can give her. I want Mrs. Burgess to take her."

While Adele passed a few days with her baby in the hospital I was in touch with the attorney for the baby's father. On the phone I reached a most thankful individual, relieved that he could deal at last with an agency. The father sent his blessings, his background data, his admission of paternity and consent for adoption. He also sent four thousand dollars. Adele's lawyer demanded and received half the money, which was given not for services rendered but to get rid of him. The rest went to Adele.

– – – – – – – – –

The unmarried mother is, in the public mind, a mysterious, bewildering person. She is fascinating enough to be a favorite subject in literature, the theater and in every soap opera on television. She is high drama. Even social workers, who have known hundreds of unmarried mothers, are lured on by the problems they present. Why this fascination? Is it the dichotomy of the out of wedlock pregnancy, the mother who is not a mother but a biological vehicle, the father who lives but is unknown, the pregnancy that exists but is denied, the baby born to one but the child of another?

Problem-solving social workers are trapped in situations for which they can find no clear resolution. The pieces of the human puzzle cannot be put together and questions remain unanswered. There are no absolutes in the solutions adoption agencies deal with. We are held in one human drama after another.

We must be able to adapt our approach, our vocabulary and our orientation to all kinds of expectant mothers. In Washington, for example, I was confronted by the wide-eyed country girl in her first job with the FBI, the sophisticated, confident State Department executive who knew her way around, and the panicky widow whose children were at an age to be shaken by their mother's unexplainable pregnancy. Social workers are not merely counselors in the emotional areas of out-of-wedlock pregnancies. They are also resources for finding living quarters, medical care and monetary assistance for expectant mothers. In recent years referrals to abortion clinics are included in the service.

A few women confidently handle all the arrangements for adoption without any assistance until they come with the baby to the agency's door. I remember vividly a strong and forthright mother who came to the agency carrying her twelve-hour-old infant wrapped in a heating pad cover. She had delivered him herself and was now ready for adoption. She was impatient with our concern for her and the baby.

To us there were a few untended details: the mother's physical well being, the baby's medical examination, his birth registration, the birth father's whereabouts, all the technical trivia which the disdainful mother had planned to avoid. We dismissed her waiting taxi and set to work.

The mother was astounded by the fact that her baby was no longer her private business, but a social and public concern. Up to the moment we had detained her, she had controlled and timed each stage of her pregnancy and the delivery of the baby. She disparaged the agency's authority and demands.

Clara was 26, a capable, liberated woman who worked in a Washington business firm as an executive secretary. Through diet and the restraint of elastic girdles, she had kept her pregnancy from showing, although she admitted that a member of the firm had recently remarked on her weight gain. She shared her apartment with a girl friend who was also ignorant of Clara's condition.

On Thursday morning, Clara felt fleeting pains, but went to work anyway. Her boss had a pressing report that had to be typed. By noon, the pains were stronger, regular, and coming closer together, and she took early leave of the office. When her roommate came home, Clara explained she was not feeling well and excused herself from supper. Her roommate ate alone and, told there was nothing she could do for Clara, left for a movie with a friend.

During her three hours alone, Clara gave birth to the baby, cleaned up the bed, the baby and herself, and went into a deep sleep with her son tucked under the covers. The roommate crept out silently in the morning not wanting to disturb Clara, but Clara was almost ready to go herself. She dressed herself, wrapped up the baby in towels and the heating pad cover, called into her office for sick leave, looked in the telephone directory for the address of an adoption agency, hailed a cab, and came. She planned to take it easy on Saturday and Sunday and be ready for a full day of work on Monday.

The baby was alert and in perfect health. Needless to say, he became a most determined, independent, and ornery young boy.

In usual situations, the unmarried mother came to the agency several months before the baby's birth. Medical and background history was obtained and contact with the alleged father was arranged long before the baby's arrival. The mother could thus concentrate on the final plans for the baby, which were of increasing concern to her as the time of birth approached. Pictures were taken of birth parents during early interviews. These portraits gave to the record the essence of their individuality, eventually providing perhaps the answer to their children's question, "What did my parents look like?"

During the mother's stay in the hospital the social worker again reviewed with her the plans for the newborn baby. On the third day the mother usually returned home and the baby was taken to the agency foster home. The mother had at least a month to make her final plans in uninterrupted thought, and I always encouraged her to visit her baby in the foster home before making a final decision.

If the mother kept her baby, she received help to get started, sometimes in a foster home with her baby. If adoption was her plan, her relinquishment was followed by immediate placement of the baby in his own adoptive home. If she surrendered her child with confidence in her decision, she would probably never return to the agency and we would not see her again.

Some mothers went through their pregnancies and the adoption of their children without any family member knowing. They invented amazing ruses so that they could stay away from home and their parents would suspect nothing out of the ordinary. An expectant mother might write home about having a fictitious government job which involved frequent traveling, making visits by her parents out of the question. She might use only a post office box and no address. She might even remain in the same city as her parents, but pretend to be elsewhere. By mailing a letter enclosing her own to a postmaster in a distant spot, she would correspond with her parents through letters mailed and stamped from another city.

In some cases a mother's desire for secrecy was understandable. One could empathize with older unmarried mothers who had established their independence and did not wish to burden elderly parents with the knowledge of their pregnancies. Some had crude and destructive parents whom they feared. Others had been warned by their parents that the consequences of their behavior would lead to pregnancy. Pride kept them from revealing that the parental admonitions had been ignored, and the consequences the parents had foreseen had been realized. Most common was the young pregnant girl whose parents represented to her a standard of rectitude that she felt she had destroyed. Her father and mother were her conscience and her example. Her sense of guilt in being pregnant out of wedlock was related to them rather than to the innocent victim, the baby. But too many young girls, instead of seeking parental reassurance, turned away from home to find help elsewhere.

I managed to persuade some young pregnant mothers to tell their parents of their plight by pointing out that their parents had had years of sexual experience and would not be horrified. I found it amusing to witness their utter surprise when their parents were supportive.

Several pregnant teenagers I counseled were technically virgins. Interestingly, they did not feel burdened with guilt as most other young girls. To them their pregnancies had been mistakes. They had not "given in." Their hymens were still intact. Perhaps guilt in the sex act is less common today, but it dominated the thinking of young pregnant girls twenty years ago.

Social workers are limited in the time they have for counseling. Although two or three months is a very short period for therapy, a woman's insight is enhanced by her pregnancy. In her isolation her defenses fall away and her sensitivity grows. It is an optimum time for change. Yet it is foolhardy for the social worker to delve too deeply, for the mother must think about the arrangements for the baby and not dwell entirely on herself. Psychoanalysis may follow an out-of-wedlock pregnancy with great benefit, but it is best undertaken after the mother makes final arrangements for her child.

One mother wrote during the period of counseling, "People often wander through the greater portion of their lives without ever noticing that even the smallest occurrences can be wonderful and exciting. Even the pain and shame and sorrow that necessarily enter every life can become edifying experiences if one only allows them to be. We bring on our own destruction as influential personalities by simply forgetting the perpetual wonder of the fact that we exist at all. This remarkable fact should be enough to make us hold to every feeling and experience and savor it well so that it will not simply slip by and be forgotten."

Counseling for the disheartened clients has to be hopeful, encouraging, and constructive. The social worker must help her client look beyond the immediate moment into future years, to visualize the baby not merely as a cute infant being cared for by a nurse or foster mother but as a toddler, school child and teenager for whom she alone might be responsible. Adoption is not, of course, the only solution to out-of-wedlock pregnancies, and a social worker who presses adoption on her clients is not worthy of her profession.

I found some mothers physically and psychologically unable to give up their newborn infants. They tried to manage alone with their babies, but often returned months later, broken and pathetic, to relinquish them after all.

The tragedy for the young mother who keeps her baby with the notion that she will have a live doll to play with begins when her negative two-year-old begins to assert himself. She is unprepared for the responsibilities of parenthood and comes to realize that she is incapable of caring for her child. Although she may now feel that adoption would have been a better plan for both of them, it is difficult for her to imagine giving up her child after their months together. Yet a few mothers do place their children in adoption after babyhood. What would have been for these mothers an experience of temporary sadness during the baby's infancy becomes one of overwhelming loss charged with guilt.

For mothers who cannot bear the final separation of relinquishing their children for adoption, yet who cannot care for them either, there is an alternative solution in a novel arrangement: Open Adoption. This is not really a new practice. It has been a custom among black families for generations, but without the legal backing of the modern form. In Open Adoption a child is legally adopted by a couple who are given complete care and custody of him. Yet contact with his birth mother is not cut off. She may visit her child and be known by him as the birth mother. Yet in the security of the adoptive home, the adopting parents, as the constant ones, will almost inevitably become the true parents in the child's eyes.

Many mothers keep their babies for neurotic and vindictive reasons which they do not fully understand. Their motives are self-serving: to show up their conservative parents, to compete with married sisters who have no children, to punish their boyfriends, the fathers of their children, by making them pay child support, to demonstrate to the world that they do not care what people think of them.

A young, unmarried mother who keeps her baby needs to make plans with her family, preferably in the quiescent time before the baby is born. Such mothers cannot raise their children without their families' participation. The children cannot grow up in vacuums and the mothers need to know how their families might react to their keeping the babies before they decide to try to "make it on their own." For these reasons, I tried to bring about reunions between the young unmarried mothers and their parents as soon as possible. Even if adoption was planned, I felt the pregnant girls needed to share the events with someone in the family with whom they could talk as the years went by.

As their pregnancies progress, the majority of unmarried mothers begin to think in terms of their babies rather than themselves. The more mature the mother, the sooner she considers the baby's welfare. Though mature mothers were in a better position to keep their babies, most of them, in my experience, chose adoption.

A few mothers I knew denied any feeling for their unborn babies until after delivery, when, like a tide, their emotions overwhelmed them. Those mothers who had set aside any plans but adoption before the birth often made a complete switch and kept their babies afterwards. They functioned first by denial of feelings and then by impulsive reaction, allowing themselves no time for reflective judgment.

Pregnancy out of wedlock is a particularly isolating and lonely experience. One mother put it quite clearly when she said, "Even in the busy, affectionate atmosphere of my 'wage home' I feel as though I am completely isolated and withdrawn from human affairs in which I previously participated so eagerly and freely. The fear that I will meet someone familiar who must not know and the reluctance to form new connections inhibit my activities until I feel as if I were in a different *little* world of my own."

The unmarried mother's tie to her baby is often strengthened by her isolation. Lonely young mothers cling to their infants as possessions they will never lose. Secluded in hospital maternity wards they are alone and emotionally helpless.

One such mother I first saw in the hospital after she had given birth to her baby. She poured out her story to me. Unable to marry the father of her baby, she had fled to Chicago where she felt she would not be found. On arrival she had gone to the Traveler's Aid desk and had been given the name of an adoption agency. As she left, an older woman saw her and offered to take her home and give her room and board in repayment for housework. The innocent girl felt lucky to have stumbled upon this magnanimous woman.

After a few weeks a stream of strange couples came to call. The girl was brought in for inspection, questioned briefly and dismissed. She had stumbled into an undercover black market operation. She escaped however and made her way to the agency. She was now a very frightened girl who wanted more than anything to protect her baby against the big city and the people in it.

In the hospital she poured out her anguished feelings to me: "My baby is part of me. How can I give up part of myself? I hated for him to be born and have him leave me even though I couldn't seem to wait until I got my figure back. Now I wouldn't care, just so I could keep him always. When I was first pregnant I was all against my baby. Now I am all for him. It took a live thing to make me see. Maybe I could still get married and keep him. How can I let him go? I want him to have a lot of love. Will he be loved? Will he be safe?"

Talking it out relieved her frantic confusion. Ultimately she chose to surrender her son for adoption and returned to her home, no longer the girl who had left four months before but a mother who hoped someday that her son would find her.

People in general and doctors in particular think social workers are cruel in advocating that an unmarried mother see her child before making a decision for adoption. They say, "If she sees the baby, she will never want to give him up." This is the very reason why I encouraged mothers to see their babies before making irreversible decisions. If a mother is so uncertain that merely viewing the child would change her mind, she is not ready to relinquish him forever.

I am reminded of a long distance phone call I received from a mother who had surrendered her baby two years before I joined the agency. She pictured her daughter wasting away in an orphanage. The mother told me that she had married and the birth of another daughter had renewed thoughts of her first. She was overwhelmed by the conviction that she had abandoned her first child. She was unable to sleep, attend her new baby, or respond to her husband.

I told her I knew the child had been adopted and promised to find out more. I located the young couple who had adopted the child. In compassion and goodwill for the birth mother, they gave me a detailed account of their daughter's wondrous ways, her appearance, her grace and beauty. A week later, I was able to relay to the mother all I had been told. She had already come out of despondency with grateful relief, just to know her baby had been adopted. She asked over and over, "What does she look like?" and was pleased by the apparent resemblance to her second child. She struggled to explain: "You see, Mrs. Burgess, I never once laid eyes on my baby. I never saw her. I never held her even once."

Having lived with her baby *in utero* for nine months, having felt her turns and her thrusts, having labored and given birth to her but not to have looked at her was, for this sensitive mother, abandonment without love. If with love she had held and blessed her child, she could then have surrendered her for adoption without the burden of future guilt.

A world of difference exists between unmarried mothers in their teens and older women in their twenties in their emotional responses to motherhood. The young girl's occasional excess of lamentation is soon replaced by conversational chatter as she boasts to her girl friends of her prowess in having had a baby. An older woman does not take her pregnancy or her baby lightly. Chronologically and emotionally she is ready for motherhood. If in her first panic she bypasses abortion, she may become one of those I observed over and over again who, through her experience, grew in depth and perception. Many unmarried mothers matured in nine short months into women of compassion and understanding.

It is most unusual if the father of an expected baby is not aware of the pregnancy. He is usually the first one told. If he later disappears or drops out of the mother's life he was at least there at the beginning in a relationship of affection if not abiding love. His pregnant girlfriend, more tenacious in her love, often clings to remembrances of the past and trusts that he will reappear to claim her and their baby.

The emotions of the deserted mother-to-be are best told by one of them: "Perhaps he did truly love me but we don't express our emotions on the same level. I think now he is one of those people who never feels anything very deeply. He has left me with nothing except the physical reminder of my love, his child growing within me, and even this I must relinquish for the sake of the existing social order. I must give away so much of myself and acquire a new personality. All this I must do alone. Alone is the key word, in all my feelings and expressions of emotion. I don't cry. The sensations are too big and tears mean nothing. They are a good outlet for lesser emotions but they do nothing to ease the heartache which affects me during my waking hours and even more during the hours of sleep. Each morning I awake feeling emotionally exhausted from the dreams and visions of him which invariably come to me. My words can only be words to ordinary people, but to those women who have lived through a pregnancy and who have been unable to forget their love, my words will mean much."

This mother experienced the ultimate in rejection losing the two humans closest to her, her lover and her baby. This was the situation in the majority of cases of the mature unmarried mothers I knew. These women clung to thin threads of evidence that their male friends still cared.

I spent hours with mothers trying to help them interpret what had transpired in their relationships. The evidence was usually there to see but hard for mothers to accept. Holding on to vain faith had a disintegrating effect upon a mother as she approached parturition. She sometimes held to one last hope, that the sight of the baby might change the father's mind. It almost never did.

A small minority of mothers were indifferent to the fathers of their babies. They may have had brief affairs with them or were currently in love with other men. The majority had had a steady relationship with one man over a long period of time. Some of these women tried to force marriage by becoming pregnant.

For the older single woman, sufficiently established to support her baby, losing her lover did not necessarily mean she must lose her baby too. It was painful for me to witness the surrender of babies by many of these grown women, lacking the courage to face their relatives and friends. I remember one forty-year-old mother, in whom I tried to inculcate the courage to keep her son, who went elsewhere to place him in adoption because I had evidently made her feel ashamed.

When the unmarried mother signs a relinquishment of parental rights for her child, the weight of the sober moment descends upon every witness to it. One can only react with silent reflection. I often found it necessary to allow myself several days of emotional adjustment between the sorrows of the unmarried mother in surrendering her baby and the elation of the adopting parents in adopting him.

The circumstances which made adoption seem necessary then are now the circumstances that make abortion seem justifiable. For example: the unmarried woman whose pregnancy is unaccepted by parents and associates, the wife pregnant by a man other than her husband, the alien servant threatened by deportation, the woman carrying her priest confessor's child, the white girl pregnant by her black schoolmate, and the crippled woman who cannot care for her infant.

There is a world of difference in the woman one month pregnant and in the same woman with her one-month-old living infant. In the first month of gestation her desire to rid herself of a problem pregnancy is negative and self-serving. Nine months later the same woman will have grown to think in positive terms about her child and welcome him to life. The option of abortion does not exist for all. One wonders whether those who go through with their pregnancies have gained or lost. In saving themselves the pain of relinquishing their children for adoption are women who abort less haunted?

After mothers surrender their babies for adoption they often seek sympathy from those still closest to their loss, the birth fathers. In several of my cases, a second pregnancy resulted from these reunions. The second confinements were more tragic for the mothers than the first. One illegitimate baby might be excused as a mistake of innocence, but with a second, the mother shares society's view of her as a fallen woman. When I encountered such cases, I managed to have the two siblings placed in the same home, much to the joy of the adopters. One birth mother was comforted by the conviction that God had given her a second child purposely to companion the first in his adoptive home. The solace for mothers having siblings grow up together was also expressed by unmarried mothers who had twins.

Some ambivalent mothers felt that they atoned for wrongdoing in the personal sacrifice of giving up their children. The thought that they were abandoning their children was unstated but lingering, and they saw adoption as inevitable.

Grace was an eye-catching female with a lovely but bland face on which no flicker of pleasure seemed ever to have shown. She did not have much to be happy about. Endowed with inordinate sexual attractiveness, she had had to run away from home at 14, making her way from job to job. At 18 she was the hostess in a Washington restaurant. Her pregnancy was just one more unlucky occurrence which she accepted as her fate.

Counseling appeared trivial for a young girl so old in her knowledge and so inert in her acceptance of the hard world she knew. She lived her life day by day without enthusiasm. She viewed adoption in the same spirit, hoping but not trusting that her child would have a better life than she could give. She was not rejecting her baby. She had already rejected herself.

Her tiny body nurtured and gave birth to a strong vigorous boy, as male as she was female. But he was born without optic nerves. We anticipated a long search for a family who would adopt a blind child. Grace was told the medical facts as well as our plan to find a family for the baby despite his handicap.

"You won't have to," she said. "Now I have a right to keep him." With what trepidation I watched her departure, her pocketbook jammed with referrals to medical clinics, apartments for rent, agencies for the blind, and her arms weighted down with bottles, diapers, blankets, and her infant son wrapped cocoon-like against the winter cold.

A month later she called to report that she had rented a room in a suburb where the baby could be outdoors. She had hired a baby sitter to care for him while she worked. She had made an appointment with the Lighthouse, an agency for the blind. Six months later she called again. Everything was going well and she was engaged to be married.

The timbre of her voice had changed. Beneath her spiritless, empty beauty, a courageous woman was emerging. Growing in responsibility for her blind son, she was awakened to the pleasures of a purposeful life.

An unmarried mother, going into hiding during her pregnancy, expects that once the baby is born and she no longer fears being seen, she will enter the world again with her troubles over. But when, through congenital misfortune, adoption is not possible, the mother, of necessity, becomes the publicly acknowledged parent of her illegitimate baby. One case illustrates how shallow the artifices of pretense appear when life itself is in jeopardy.

A sensitive young college sophomore had come to Washington from Idaho, leaving her campus as her pregnant condition began to show. Only the baby's father knew of her predicament. Unable to persuade him to marry her, she went as far away as she could to place her baby in adoption. Dreading the reaction of her family and friends. she was humiliated and fearful.

The child was born with multiple defects: his intestines were scrambled, his heart had a septal defect, his anus was closed, and his malformed skull spewed brains onto the back of his neck. But he lived. Eager young interns in the university hospital where he was born were fascinated by the unusual anomalies in the infant and were challenged to prevent his death. The doctors triumphed and the small maimed creature was discharged to his stunned mother.

An institutional life awaited him. His mother had no funds for private care. Local public institutions would not take the responsibility of financing his care. Idaho, the state of his mother's residence, would have to assume the costs. And his mother would have to take him there herself.

Why was this harsh burden suddenly visited upon an unmarried mother who had gone to such lengths to avoid exposure? Because the child must belong to somebody. Otherwise who would give permission for surgery? Who would be given notice of illness or death? And who would bury the child?

In preparation for the trip west, the agency could merely prepare food, clothing, and a basket to hold the baby. It could arrange for an agency at the other end to meet them and ease the transfer of the baby to the state institution.

It was the mother who carried the true burden, a cross much heavier to bear than the lighter one she had discarded, that of maintaining the good name of her family and herself.

Most adoptive mothers expressed sympathy with the plight of the unmarried mother. Some expressed it thus: "There but for the grace of God go I." Some mothers assumed a special obligation to be good parents for the sake of the birth mothers who sacrificed themselves to give them children. Others felt the idea of obligation to the unmarried mother was sentimental nonsense. "You can't owe twice as much to your children because they are adopted." One mother thought emotional identity with birth mothers was unrealistic, but another mother identified in a different way, dying her hair to match the red heads of all four of the birth mothers of her adopted children. And then there were the adoptive mothers who directly and simply remembered their children's birth mothers in their prayers.

4 BIOLOGICAL FATHERS

HARVEY WAS AN ENSIGN IN THE NAVY on home leave when his son was born. During his last months at sea, he had fantasized reunion with his girlfriend and an immediate wedding, for his bride would already be six months pregnant. The wedding did not take place. Virginia had found another love in Harvey's absence. Harvey, in agitated hope, became a beggar for attention. To Virginia who was strong and willful, Harvey appeared weak and sniveling, a man she would never want to marry. She made plans for the adoption of their unborn baby.

Harvey was crushed, clinging doggedly to the thought that after the baby was born Virginia would change her mind. She did not change, but he did.

The baby was born and taken into foster care at the mother's request. Frustrated and angry, the now awesome father demanded his son. Having lost his girl, Harvey was not going to lose his baby too. He obtained a writ of habeas corpus which was served on the agency. No response was necessary however for the five-day-old infant, with critical heart failure, had been taken from the agency to the hospital. There, on neutral ground, Harvey became a parent equal to the place of the mother. For five days, he scarcely left the hospital, badgering doctors, nurses and attendants for the latest reports. He prayed for a miracle and talked to his son through the double glass of the nursery and the incubator separating him from the child.

Harvey prevailed upon a visiting priest, touched by the father's anxiety, to christen the baby and give him his father's name. Thus the baby of a Protestant mother became a Catholic and was acknowledged as the legitimate child of his father. The hospital staff had no idea that Harvey had assumed the role of parent without legal rights to do so.

Virginia, recovering from her delivery, isolated herself, and made inquiries about her son by phone. In turmoil and remorse she could not face Harvey. But she had to make one trip to the hospital for only she, the single legal parent, could release the infant, dead of heart disease, to a funeral home.

In the end the baby became if not his father's legal son at least his spiritual one. The serviceman father saw to it that his child was buried at Arlington Cemetery.

— — — — — — — — — —

Birth fathers have so infrequently contested the adoption of their illegitimate children that they have never been considered major threats to the execution of adoptions. However, adoption workers can no longer ignore them.

On April 3, 1972, the Supreme Court made a decision which jolted adoption workers and turned the usual adoption procedures into chaos. The ruling in the case of *Stanley* v. *Illinois* found that an unwed father has rights equal to those of the married father.

The case came about upon the death of an unmarried mother, whose illegitimate children were taken into custody by an Illinois welfare department against the father's will. The Illinois court had contended that the father, not having married the mother, did not have the right of choice in the matter of his illegitimate children. The Supreme Court held that the father had been denied due process and was entitled to a hearing. Thus unwed fathers were accorded the same rights as married fathers with equal protection under the law.

Social workers, who had previously been content to ignore unmarried fathers, were confronted with the necessity of notifying alleged fathers of the anticipated adoptions of their offspring.

Locating the elusive father is laborious work for the agencies, and sometimes impossible. A relinquishment of parental rights lacking a father's signature will not be accepted in court without clear evidence that every effort has been made to find him. Children are kept in temporary foster homes longer and longer as social workers search for their fathers.

Richard Barker, an astute lawyer, had anticipated the Supreme Court decision by thirty years. In the agency he founded in Washington, identification of the alleged father was required of expectant mothers seeking adoption. As case worker and director of The Barker Foundation and later of the Peirce-Warwick Adoption

Service, I had already had twenty years of experience in tracking down alleged fathers when the requirements became law.

The purpose of my agencies' search for fathers was not solely to grant them notice of their expectant fatherhood, as the case of *Stanley* v. *Illinois* now requires, but to get from them medical and social data for the adoption. In my thinking the rights of the father for notification are subordinate to the rights of the child for a known parental heritage. In most agencies the entire absence of paternal history is in marked contrast to the full medical and social history of the mother. One would have to assume that the sperm's contribution was not significant.

It took strong conviction and persistence to track down some of the absent men. My searches led me from Maine to California, to Korea, Vietnam, Germany, Greece, Turkey, Iran, Mexico, Argentina, Zambia, and Tanzania. Most of the fathers in distant places could do no more than fill out background forms on family and medical history, and sign statements consenting to adoption. Those living close to Washington came to the office for interviews.

Personal interviews were, of course, more satisfactory than forms returned to us by mail. When we failed to gain the cooperation of the father we had to depend on the mother to recall facts about him, an amazingly poor source of information, I found.

The legal forms the fathers signed gave their consent to adoption and also gave them the option of admitting or denying paternity. Sometimes only by being able to deny paternity would the father give us the information we asked for. Denying paternity was a ruse. The papers were signed with tongue in cheek, usually on advice of lawyers, against the possibility of the fathers being held liable for child support if the mothers kept their babies after all.

When attorneys entered the scene, unmarried mothers acquired the role of seducers and fathers became victims about to be ripped off. The male defense in or out of court, was to produce several companions who claimed they could as well have fathered the baby. Threatened with this prospect, few unmarried mothers had the temerity to seek child support. Using blood tests as proof of paternity was not satisfactory either. They indicate only what man is *not* the father and do not show positive proof who is.

I never encouraged an unmarried mother to depend upon child support from the father, so uncertain were her chances of success. Rather I encouraged her to face the more realistic possibility that if she kept her baby, the responsibility would be hers alone. I know a few happy instances in which a mother was granted support voluntarily from the baby's father, resulting in a relationship similar to an amicable divorce.

If the father is found, he may fail to honor the mother's choice of adoption and refuse to sign the papers of relinquishment. One such case, which occurred before the *Stanley* v. *Illinois* decision, illustrates the possible complications.

An expectant mother in her thirties applied to the agency to place her baby in adoption. She had left her lover in Chicago and come home to her family in Washington. Her boyfriend did not know she was pregnant until, with the mother's consent, we notified him and asked for his family history.

He arrived in Washington shortly after the baby's birth. Cooperating with us in giving information we wanted for the adoption, he then asked to see the baby. It is a common request and we brought the baby to the office for him to see. The infant was attractive, appealing, and a son. The father was opposed in principle to adoption and to the adoption of this child in particular. He declared, "If his mother doesn't want him, I do."

During the pregnancy this mother had come to feel the baby to be hers rather than theirs, and she wished to exercise the right of having her son adopted.

The father protested that a child belongs with a true birth parent; if not with the mother, then with the father. He wanted to take the baby home to his wife to be raised with his other four children. His wife, however, was unaware of the prolonged affair and of the child who had been born as a result.

The mother received the proposal with horror. She protested his right to subject her child to such an uncertain future. She saw belatedly how her lover had neglected his family for her, and she could not trust him to be more responsible with her child. Furthermore, knowing where the child lived would be a constant torment to her. She insisted that since she felt ill-equipped to raise her child, she wanted him to be brought up in the security of a stable adoptive home.

The angry father demanded release of the child to him and threatened a lawsuit. But before he could act the mother took the child away and placed him in an adoptive family through an agency outside the jurisdiction where the suit was to be filed.

Granted a hearing, this father might well have lost his case but meanwhile the child would have passed many vital months in limbo.

"P.F." or "putative father" is a designation still used in social agencies for the father of the child born out of wedlock. The age old term depicts not only the illusive nature of paternity but also the distrust social workers, aligned in sympathy with the unmarried mother, felt toward him. The assumption used to be that men took advantage of innocent girls and then disappeared to let them bear the children in shame. The establishment of maternity homes where victimized women could be hidden and protected was liberally supported by commiserating socialites and deprecators of the male sex.

Social workers today know that few unmarried mothers are innocent victims of male aggression. Rather they are victimized because they are female and possess the unique function of their sex, child bearing. If they were the male partner they too would seek escape from responsibility and burden. Many today do just that in aborting their unborn offspring.

Because of the paternal identification policy of the agencies where I have worked, I have had the unique opportunity of knowing many "putative fathers." Search for the father, unless the mother preferred to reach him herself, was the agency's task. If we failed to find him or to gain his cooperation in giving us medical and social information, that was considered our fault, and the mother's request for adoption service was not rejected.

We were amazingly successful. Only a few fathers lived up to the name of "alleged" or "putative." In a few instances I was aware that a mother may have substituted a friendly male companion for the real parent, or that there might be a choice between fathers. But the vast majority of biological fathers of over nine hundred children were located and willingly identified themselves. In the sixties, during a period of five years, I was able to reach by phone, letter, and personal meetings 299 fathers out of the 314 I sought.

Locating fathers was the first step. Gaining their confidence and cooperation followed. In the main, fathers were sincerely sorry for the plight of the women they had impregnated and wanted to help them, if not with funds, at least by giving the agency the information required for adoption. Hesitant fathers were motivated to active participation when warned that without their cooperation adoption would be improbable.

In general, I found that white fathers cared for their babies to a greater or lesser degree depending on their attachment to the mothers. If they renounced marriage, they tended to favor adoption for their own protection as well as that of the babies.

Black fathers, on the other hand, took greater pride in their procreants regardless of the feelings they had for the mothers. Many found it unconscionable that a mother could give up her baby and opposed adoption in all situations. Gaining the cooperation of such fathers was more difficult. Sometimes even when they came to the office and answered the questions about family background for the purpose of adoption, they refused to sanction adoption itself by signing any papers of consent.

White fathers, unlike their black brothers, were worried that the pregnancies, if disclosed, would dishonor them. Expectant fathers bringing these fears with them to the office were foreign students afraid of deportation, teenaged sons alarmed lest mothers find out, playboy romeos dismayed at being caught, military school undergraduates fearful of being expelled, and guilty husbands apprehensive of their wives' suspicions. There were also pleased young boys awed that their wild oats had actually germinated.

To each expectant father his problems appeared unique. To the social worker his problems were a familiar repetition of many previous cases. The longer her experience, the greater was her facility in weighing the factors of each case and in predicting the outcome.

The putative fathers whom I interviewed ranged in age from fourteen to fifty-eight, from spontaneous youth to abashed middle aged.

The fourteen-year-old dumbfounded his parents, his girl's parents, and the social workers in the adoption agency and the maternity home by spiriting away his expectant girlfriend from the maternity home as she began her labor. He drove her one hundred miles through a winter night in a collapsing car he had put together out of parts from junked vehicles. The teenaged mother was delivered at their home town hospital only half an hour after arrival there. The boy knew that if the baby was born at home all the neighbors would know and both families, no longer able to deny the pregnancy, would relent and allow them to be married. He had broken through the powerful web which the adult world had spun about his fate. A minor child, subject to adult decisions, he became a father and husband with one quick stroke of defiance.

The fifty-eight-year-old had never been married. When he found his woman friend was pregnant, he panicked at the thought of being a father, even more so of being a family man. He arranged for the expectant mother to have an abortion but she refused to go through with it. She had been born out of wedlock herself and decided to keep the baby as her mother had kept her.

Despairing of this recalcitrant female, the father made an appointment with the adoption agency. I had learned, through repeated experience, that when an expectant father made the first call to the agency the mother was merely placating him in coming and was not sincerely interested in adoption. Events moved along as expected. The baby was delivered at a private hospital and the mother took the baby home. She moved in with her neurotic, despondent mother, and the three generations of illegitimate females lived together inharmoniously.

There was one bright spot. The father, who refused to marry, nevertheless supported his baby and became a surrogate father, husband, and son-in-law.

Married fathers, by law, are presumed to be parents of all the children born to their wives, even if there is reason to doubt their actual paternity. Therefore a woman separated from her husband and pregnant by another man has to get consent for adoption from her husband. This was an embarrassing and sometimes terrifying prospect for a mother who had other children in the marriage, and feared to lose them because of the evidence of her adultery. I never knew a case in which this happened. Husbands were usually sympathetic and cooperative.

In the cases of married men who fathered children of women other than their wives, the story was different. They were reluctant participants, dragged to the agency by their expectant girl friends. Before abortion became the easy way out in such situations, adoption of the baby was the usual solution. One became sensitive to the tangled relationships of these cases and learned to handle them with care. By comparison, unmarried fathers were easy.

In coming to the office for an interview, fathers presented themselves in various self-conscious ways: boastful, restless, cautious, and disdainful. Relieved to find that we were neither moralists out to reform them nor misers seeking their money, they usually relaxed quickly and shared with us the information we needed for the proper placements of their babies. The measure of their trust was confirmed by their willingness, in almost every instance, to have their pictures taken before they left the office. The colored Polaroid portraits were placed in the files with those of the mothers.

Counseling expectant fathers involved reassurance and understanding rather than decision making, for the fathers in most cases accepted the plan of adoption as final. As pregnancies progressed, fathers became more assured of the good sense of the original decision, while mothers became less convinced of the desirability of adoption. A mother's continuing devotion to the father of her baby seemed an almost universal experience. She wanted him to marry her, which was the only way she felt able to keep her baby. I noted much greater variation in the father's feelings for the mother.

In the usual case, a father was seen only once. He left the interview with a sense of a duty done and of relief that a professional adult was taking over a problem he wished to be rid of. It was an unusual case in which a father sought counseling for himself. I restricted counseling to problems directly related to the pregnancy, leaving fathers free to live happily with their neuroses or to seek help elsewhere.

Counseling revealed fathers in emotional confusion and fearful of commitment. Some felt guilty for being responsible for the pregnancy and perplexed by their lack of feeling for the expectant mother. There were those whose relationships had been casual and others whose original devotion had dissolved with knowledge of the pregnancies. One might be remorseful that he had taken advantage of a naive woman while another might think the pregnancy a deliberate attempt by the mother to force marriage. Some who were deeply in love were unable to marry, and others were too young to consider it.

Counseling many student fathers from the Near East and Africa, where men have absolute authority in the family, required giving them a course in the customs and laws of the United States. Not only was adoption strange to them but a mother's right to her baby was odd. One father from Africa, with permission from the mother, did manage to take his child home to Africa with him to become a member of his family's tribal group.

The social worker often became the bridge between a reluctant father, unable to confess his plans to decamp, and a mother anticipating an imminent marriage to him. Fearful of hurting her the guilt-ridden father found it easier to talk to the objective social worker. It was left to the social worker to ease the blow for the mother and to try to interpret the father's motivations and intentions. Many a father imposed a cruel wrong by waiting until after the baby's birth to tell the mother he wanted out.

I remember one faint-hearted expectant father who gave freely of his sympathy but never *did* declare what his intentions were. He was a middle-aged bachelor whose summer romance had resulted in the pregnancy of a sensitive and unworldly widow. He left her with the impression of his continued interest, to which she clung in desperation. However, marriage eluded her, and far along in her pregnancy the widow sent her children away for a long "visit" to relatives while she sequestered herself in a one-room apartment to await her delivery. Despondent and terrified when she had no letter from her lover, she was hopeful yet uncertain when she did hear from him.

As a devoted and experienced mother, she found the thought of giving up her baby overwhelming. Time, hanging over her like a shroud, ran out and she finally gave birth. The lover, thinking to spare her grief and himself the annoyance of an angry scene, still evaded her plea for marriage. After the delivery, the mother lay in her hospital bed with the baby she would soon lose at her side and, on the table, a beautiful bouquet of spring flowers with a congratulatory note from the absent father.

Flashes of other episodes come to mind:

The suspension from preparatory school of an expectant father whose headmaster expelled him for the same number of months as his teenaged girlfriend was forced into seclusion by her pregnancy.

A quiet interview with an expectant father under the shelter of an elevated automobile, as the father-mechanic shot grease into the underpinnings of the vehicle above us and we soberly reviewed his life story.

A brawl between a vindictive mother and myself for the possession of an admission of paternity, signed by the father, which she wished to use against him. Though 35 years older, I proved stronger. The poor, crazed mother was quickly exhausted, having given birth only four days before.

A carefully disguised registered letter, "for his eyes only," mailed to an alleged father in Argentina which was reciprocated with a grandiose acknowledgment of paternity, a document in elegant script, notarized with a colorful seal and a red satin ribbon across its face.

A transported young father awkwardly grasping his infant at the waist, while clothes and blankets slipped upward and scrawny legs dangled bare below. He was blind to all but the baby's face, whose features he tried to memorize. The young man asked to be left alone for a last communion with his son.

A jolting first view of a black-haired Oriental infant, whose heritage was supposed to be Anglo-Saxon, requiring a quick shift from alleged father Chandler to father Chang. The second father was intrigued by the disclosure of his paternity, but was penniless and could not have provided the financial support already donated by putative father number one.

A packet of family background forms and legal papers sent airmail to Vietnam and returned unclaimed. The father to whom I had addressed the letter had been killed in combat one week before his son's birth.

The horror on the face of the security-agent-father when I raised the camera to take his picture.

The tender words of a teenage father describing his thrill and amazement when he felt the first movements of his baby within the mother's womb. Too young to support a family, he was old enough to exalt in the wonder of life.

A father, who took precautions to restrict the number of children within his marriage, telling of his resolution to advance his race by producing unlimited illegitimate offspring outside his marriage. He had already fathered two other infants brought to the agency for adoption.

The curious stares of the rescue squad staff as, unidentified, I waited in their office for the return of an uncooperative alleged father from a local disaster. He was their chief.

A couple, ceremoniously passing under crossed swords, getting married upon the groom's graduation from military school. Unknown to all others, the bride and groom had relinquished their baby for adoption two weeks before so that the father would not be expelled for immoral conduct unbefitting an officer.

A devoted and rejected suitor's relief in being able to marry his girl after all when she was cast aside by her lover, who left her pregnant and alone. The couple thought they could forget the biological father and keep the baby as theirs together. But so much did the baby girl resemble her birth father that she became a ghostly presence in the home. Only through adoption of the child, by other parents did the marriage survive.

The most difficult cases for me were those of married couples, who saw having a baby as their only problem. They thought if I would only take the baby they could live happily ever after.

With all the married couples who asked to have their babies adopted, the plan was initiated by the husband and carried through by the force of his domination. The reasoned arguments against keeping the baby were initially accepted by both parents. After the birth, the emotionally awakened mother was in turmoil for several weeks until she finally acquiesced to her husbands demands. If a change of plan occurred it was the baby rather than my counseling that did it. It was hard for me to endure the inhuman detachment of these couples and the short range view their action exhibited, even when a father explained it to me in a letter.

"Our marriage has been a very happy one, disturbed only by the current pregnancy. I do not feel that the pregnancy and the idea of a child would be any threat to the happiness of our marriage directly, but the pregnancy itself has had a very negative effect on my wife's happiness and mental outlook and, if it were necessary to keep the child, I am sure the effect would be very harmful."

In this case, as in all cases of married couples, I refused to take the baby without their seeing her. I felt that the security of the adoption, should they later change their minds, required it. As I dressed the baby on the mother's hospital bed, the mother made rueful glances toward the baby and the father turned his back. I often wonder what their feelings and those of other married couples have been as the years go by. The babies no doubt are doing well. Are the parents?

I might have had something to do with the decision of one married couple who finally kept their baby. Edna and Albert Barnes, an idealistic white couple who saw as their life's work the uplifting of minority peoples. In the 1950's, before it became commonplace, the Barneses became revolutionaries for the Negro cause.

They were well read, well educated intellectuals. Albert was a graduate student and part-time waiter; Edna a full-time secretary. The pregnancy was unplanned and a shock to both of them. Adoption seemed a logical solution. They did not see how they could continue their way of life, attending meetings, planning strategy, printing pamphlets, soliciting signatures, protest marching, picketing, and even being jailed if they had to tend to a baby. A baby was a small venture, pretty common in the human scene, and not to be compared to the earth-shaking enterprises they had in mind. Was it so illogical that one white baby might be sacrificed for the welfare of hundreds of black children?

Sympathetic with their idealistic aims and their youthful enthusiasm, I listened and probed to try to learn what early conditioning underlay their decision to give their baby away. Young and self-absorbed, they were fascinated to find the pattern of their early lives revealed in their actions as adults. Both only children, Edna and Albert had rejected in disgust the values, standards and way of life of their conservative parents. But now they discovered that both of them had been denied siblings because, as their parents had put it, "children are too much trouble." Although they could understand the relationship of their parents' views to their own attitudes, that discovery was not enough to turn them from their adoption plan. It was humor that finally opened their eyes.

I pictured for them their child placed for adoption in the family of a republican banker from Mississippi.

I pictured the asset the baby would be for their cause, backpacked in sleet and snow, drawing sympathy and attention, as they picketed with him down Pennsylvania Avenue to the White House.

I pictured the possibility of their giving birth to an Abraham Lincoln who, because he was not raised by them, might waste his talents in business. The Barneses came to love our sessions together, and seemed to be moving away from adoption. But of course it was the baby himself who really won them over. They proudly named him Frederick Dubois Barnes—Frederick for Frederick Douglass and Dubois for W.E.B. Dubois.

The final item on the agency's background forms which expectant fathers filled in asked this question: "We wish to place your child in the most suitable home for him. What are your wishes or special desires for your child?" The usual answer was "Whatever the mother wishes." But there were occasionally other comments reflecting the father's interest:

"I only want my child to be happy."

"A chance to learn to think critically about life in a family with strong, unsuperficial and (hopefully) religious life, Episcopal, Roman

Catholic, or Greek Orthodox. Also plenty of love and affection with people who are concerned about others and are sensitive to them."

"An active home where sports are of particular interest. The mother and I are both above average in intelligence and would therefore want our child to have a chance for a good education. The child should be very adept in many activities which require body coordination."

"To be placed in a home where he will receive love and affection. To grow up in a healthy environment and not have to struggle to live."

"That he grow up with a strong value system that he could work with when older."

"That he be placed in a home and family of happiness."

"A well adjusted, established family."

And finally a 19-year-old student wrote, "That if at any time in the future the child wishes to contact me for any purpose, the agency give him all available information, including this form if possible, to assist him in contacting me."

5 INVOLVED GRANDPARENTS

THE TWO GRANDMOTHERS OF AN INFANT yet to be born were in combat. The paternal grandmother wanted her son, like any civilized father, to keep his baby. The maternal grandmother, insisting there would be no illegitimate grandchild in her home, wanted adoption.

The mother herself was determined to keep her baby. She was the oldest of a number of siblings, the first to break away and bring disgrace upon her strict and upwardly striving family. The baby's father, a pleasant and irresolute youth, drifted with the tide, a helpless male in the midst of three strong females doing battle.

Permission to marry had been given the seventeen-year-old expectant father by his parents, so that the couple might marry and legitimize the baby. The expectant mother, also seventeen, had been threatened with banishment if she brought the baby home. No permission for marriage was granted her. In the view of her professional family, marriage and a baby would deprive the daughter of a college education, would necessitate their support of the young couple, and would require baby care of a reluctant grandmother.

The two grandmothers refused to meet, and communicated only through third parties who passed malicious gossip back and forth. The denouement came with the arrival of the baby.

The intimidated father, both grandmothers, and the extraneous social worker confronted each other at the bedside of the newly delivered mother. Queen of all she surveyed, the mother was no longer the delinquent minor but now a manipulating woman and the only legal parent. No matter how loud the grandmothers' accusations or how vigorous the protests, the child's fate was in the hands of the mother. Relishing the contest to the end, she finally made her decision and handed the three-day-old baby to the paternal grandmother who, in surprise and relief, held the infant to her, gratified that her grandchild would be hers.

But it was not to be. After eight months, the mother, having scarcely seen the infant, demanded her child back. The paternal grandmother, who had invested her time and her love in the baby with the conviction she would have him permanently, was appalled at the thought of losing him. The power of the law finally forced the grandmother, unprotected with legal custody of the child, to give him back to the mother.

A short time later, the mother reached legal maturity and, no longer needing consent for marriage, eloped with the baby's father. The young husband joined the army to support his wife in college and his baby at the home of his mother-in-law, now reconciled to accepting the marriage and the legitimized infant.

As fate would have it, the child's father died only six months later in the service of his country. His wife and baby, widow and orphan, were financially set for life with veterans survivor's benefits. The maternal grandmother, who had so resolutely rejected her daughter, her grandson and all the paternal family, had triumphed. She now had the well-supported orphaned grandson, no longer the illegitimate offspring of a "bum," but the lone survivor of a war hero. Her daughter was receiving the much sought college education and furthermore, was unattached and free to make a suitable marriage which would bring credit to the family. The paternal grandmother, who with heartfelt sacrifice had reached out to help in the crisis, had lost both son and grandson. Where did justice lie?

— — — — — — — — — —

The arrival of a new grandchild into a family is usually a time of rejoicing. But when the baby is born out of wedlock, the scene becomes one of invective and blame, dividing family members in emotional turmoil. In anticipation of parental reaction to their illegitimate pregnancies, most unmarried expectant mothers do not share their predicament with their parents, but arrange adoption or abortion in seclusion.

An expectant mother may gain hospital admission, be delivered and relinquish her baby for adoption without her parents' knowledge, even though a parent may be named next of kin. In many states, even a pregnant girl under the age of majority does not require consent of parents for the adoption of her offspring. In other states a guardian *ad litem* is appointed by the court to represent the child of a minor. In many cases where grandparents are named as the guardians, inter-family problems explode.

Confusion abounds when the young teenager becomes a legal mother while still a dependent of her parents. Though she has a new status as mother, she is still a minor. She is old enough to become pregnant, but cannot marry without parental consent. The father of her baby may be considered competent to vote three years before he can legally take a wife without his parents' consent. Nevertheless, even a young girl of minor age gains authority as mother of her baby. If she places her baby in adoption, she returns to her parents as a minor child. If she keeps her baby, she retains the authority she gained by becoming a mother, but she loses the freedom she once had by taking on the responsibility of her child.

Parents tend to blind themselves to the evidence of pregnancy in their unmarried daughters and the daughters go through months of fear and anguish alone. One father, alarmed at his daughter's strong abdominal pains, rushed her to the hospital for what he thought would be an emergency appendectomy only to find himself a grandparent instead. In another case, a young girl, who always intended to tell her parents about her pregnancy but never found the opportune time, delivered her baby on the bathroom floor as her shocked mother entered in response to her cries for help. After the facts are revealed, the blinded parents recall evidences of pregnancy they failed to see: weight gain, odd events, passing remarks, and even hints their daughter put forth deliberately in order that her parents would know.

Once they are aware of the pregnancy, grandparents of the child about to be born almost universally defend their own and blame the other partner. The mother of a wayward son is apt to say, "My son is honorable and upstanding. He would never do such a thing." The father of a pregnant girl often defends his daughter in fiery anger: "My daughter is a good and innocent girl; she was taken advantage of and used by that no good bastard."

The social worker is seldom involved with the parents of older unmarried mothers, even when the parents are aware of adoption plans. I found that most parents wisely left the decision about the disposition of the babies to their daughters. Many offered to help if their daughters chose to keep the infants. Others, who had had years of problems with their growing girls, saw the pregnancies as just another catastrophe to live through and turned away from offering further succor.

The counseling of teenaged unmarried mothers is complex. The social workers must deal not only with the expectant mothers and fathers, but with their emotionally involved parents as well. The parents' authority over their unmarried daughters is absolute and the social workers' counsel pales by comparison. In the emotionally charged climate, social workers are frequently unable to affect rational decisions.

In my experience grandmothers more than grandfathers were often disposed to keep their grandchildren born out of wedlock. Behind the scenes, the men appeared more practical in looking ahead and anticipating future problems. Perhaps less enamored of infants than were their wives, they were less bound emotionally to the newborn babies than to their troubled teenaged daughters. They could foresee their daughters' burdened lives, their interrupted schooling, the hardship of child care and financial support. Some fathers put their feet down, forbidding their daughters to bring the babies home. They thereby determined quite simply that adoption was the only decision to be made.

Although the mother's decision for adoption might be final, some grandmothers, perhaps out of a sense of guilt in abandoning a grandchild, insisted that the least they could do was to see that the baby's birth was legitimate. Somehow, "giving the baby a name" cast out the sin of unsavory birth. A marriage was arranged for the young expectant couple, the infant, just barely born within the bonds of wedlock, was placed in adoption, the couple was then divorced, and everything was back to normal in no time. Or so thought many grandmothers, oblivious of the confusion and the hypocrisy of their actions.

When adolescent rebellion contributes to pregnancy, the direction and the outcome of the quarrel between the expectant mother and her parents is not confined to them alone. The welfare of the unborn baby, who may be the ultimate victim, is at stake. To the extent that the social worker can guide the decision in the few weeks before the birth, she owes it to the baby, as well as to the emotionally entrapped mother and grandparents, to do so. In dealing with teenage mothers whose thoughts are only of the moment, she must not be an impassive counselor, but must be assertive in presenting realistically the long-range picture on which the decision must be based.

The expectant young mother's rebellious demand for independence gives only a partial clue to the actual relationship she has with her parents. Her legal dependency on her family is absolute, and her emotional dependency encasing. The immature young mother-to-be can grow to understand her behavior and her family relationships only by separation from them. The maternity home provides an environment in which a young expectant girl may look at herself objectively and come to greater maturity in preparation for the adult decisions she must make. Instead of having her problem either covered up or flaunted in the atmosphere of her home, the expectant mother in the maternity shelter is better able to unravel the complexities of her life and to focus on the real and alternative plans for herself and her baby. The maternity home social workers are broadly experienced in the problem of unmarried mothers, and their counseling, as well as that of the adoption agency social workers, is invaluable to expectant mothers of all ages. It is a relief for most young mothers to discover in a maternity home that they are not the only ones to be pregnant out of wedlock.

Many controlling mothers do not allow their pregnant daughters to leave home, no matter how persuasive a social worker might be in promoting the benefits of separation. I cannot count the number of times I have heard the indignant reply made by expectant grandmothers to my suggestion of maternity home care for their daughters. "I wouldn't think of allowing my daughter to be in that sort of place," they say, "What kind of association would she have with all those pregnant girls?" Then they might blandly reiterate the old adage, "A girl in this sort of trouble belongs at home with her mother."

Grandmothers who have been utterly shocked by their daughters' pregnancies and have hidden the knowledge from family and friends may completely reverse themselves after the baby is born. Unable to resist the appeal of the newborn baby, they ignore the previously well laid plans and their daughters' feeble protests, and carry their grandchildren home from the hospital in triumph.

Today, when most unmarried mothers are young dependent girls, taking the baby home is more often the grandmother's decision than the daughter's. It occurs with increasing frequency as social censorship of illegitimacy wanes and the grandmothers care less what people may think. After the first joyful weeks with the new baby, the inevitable conflict between the mother and grandmother begins to appear. Although the immature young mother possesses the rights of parenthood, the grandmother carries the responsibilities. The mother not infrequently manages to slither away from the cares of motherhood into the normal carefree life of her peers, leaving the resentful grandmother to raise the child. This grim picture represents a common experience in recent years, even though, in exceptional cases, illegitimate children of young mothers are incorporated into close welcoming families with positive results.

In one extraordinary case the clash of wills between the expectant mother and grandmother reached proportions of such violence that my only thought was, "Can I save the baby?" The fatherless pregnant daughter had demanded consent for marriage from her disgusted mother. Although the young couple, both aged fifteen, had not needed permission to procreate, they now needed consent to make it legal. The grandmother refused. She guarded her daughter day and night for fear she would run away. She made the appointment with the adoption agency herself and tricked her daughter into coming to see me. My first challenge was to break down the sullen anger of the young mother-to-be at being deceived into coming. I had to align myself with the girl against her mother to inspire confidence in me. I listened endlessly to the screaming pair: the stubborn, rebellious pregnant daughter declaring she would keep her baby no matter what, and her mother threatening to send her daughter to an institution for morally delinquent girls. It took several appointments before the suspicious mother would allow me to speak to her daughter alone.

The pregnant girl was a perfect client for a maternity home but I could not bring this about. She flatly refused, saying she was not going to be "put away." Her mother was equally resistant and would not allow her daughter that far out of her sight and control. The neurotic, grasping dependency of the two women was not severable. Appalling as were her methods in dealing with her daughter, the mother's insistence on adoption of her grandchild was obviously the better choice, the only way to save the baby from the cycle of malignancy he would suffer in their hands. Alone for counseling, the expectant mother was gently propelled toward adoption. Eventually I even managed over the protests of her mother to arrange for the girl and her boyfriend to meet together for a sober review of their plans, plans which they came to see as more fantastic than real.

After the baby's birth the conflict between mother and grandmother, which I had temporarily smothered in counseling, flared anew. Although it was over the baby they fought, they were so engrossed in their own angry conflict that the baby seemed extraneous, a mere catalyst for their hostilities.

Not surprisingly, I learned at this time that the grandmother had never been married. A lonely woman, bitter and resentful, she blamed her daughter's birth for her unhappy life. As the whole story unfolded, I could feel only compassion for both mother and grandmother, shackled as they were by their isolation, their dependency and their guilty remorse.

The innocent infant was eventually rescued from his cyclonic birth family and placed in the calms of a peaceful adoptive home. If I was guilty of playing God, I am sure the Lord was on my side.

In another case, the circumstances of the mother-daughter relationship were identical but the outcome just the opposite. The daughter was forced by her mother to keep the baby. The mother was a single woman (probably never married) whose whole life was wrapped up in her only child. The daughter's attempt to escape into a love affair resulted in pregnancy with no prospect of marriage. The angry, inflexible mother believed that her daughter must bear the consequences of her wrongdoing. The overburdened grandmother worked to support her daughter and grandchild, and the young mother dropped out of school to stay home and tend the baby. The last time I saw her, the victimized young mother was passing aimlessly down the street, pausing to stare into store windows, carrying her year-old colossus on one slender hip. Consciously or unconsciously, a bitter and lonely woman thus held her daughter in inescapable bondage.

Grandparents usually suffer in silence when their children do not bring up the grandchildren as they would like. But when grandchildren are raised by single mothers, the grandparents often assume a proprietary right to supervise their grandchildren's upbringing, as they would not do if their daughters were married. Discord within families can disrupt the peaceful growth of children just as the pulling and hauling between birth and adoptive parents might if adoption did not separate them. Yet there is no corresponding protection for children kept by their mothers and caught in family feuds.

The collision between the rights of parents and of grandparents in raising a child is illustrated in one appalling case in which I was involved. Although the case is extreme, the pattern of struggle between generations within a family is not uncommon.

A young unmarried couple applied to the agency for the placement of their unborn infant in adoption. They were unable to support a child and continue their education at the same time. Living together while attending college, they planned to marry upon graduation. The paternal grandfather vowed to withdraw support of his son in college if he got married for, as a married man, the son was expected to give up his education and take on the full responsibilities of a husband and father.

A baby girl was born to the young couple and, two days before the adoption was to take place, the father's parents offered to take their granddaughter into their care until the couple graduated from college and was married. The happy pair took the baby to the local airport where the grandparents awaited them. They signed some papers and went back to school much relieved.

At the end of three years the couple graduated from college, were married and went home to claim their daughter. But the grandparents refused to give her up. They had in their possession the papers, showing the relinquishment of the child into their custody, which both parents had guilelessly signed three years before. The rival claims for the child grew into a family feud and lawyers were hired. Anticipating defeat, the grandparents kidnapped the child. They fled with her to Florida, a place of retreat used by many to escape the laws of their resident states.

The white and black grandparents of yesterday looked upon adoption in quite different ways. The white grandmother, puritanical in her WASP culture, hid her illegitimate grandchild within her family clan with a false identity, or sought adoption as a way of removing the shameful evidence. The black grandmother, on the other hand, took illegitimacy in stride as part of the human condition, and assumed at least partial care of grandchildren born out of wedlock. Losing their kin to legal adoption was not in black thinking. Black grandparents have frequently raised not only their children and grandchildren but those of poorer relatives and friends as well. The humanitarian "adoptions" of traditional black grandparents were casual and without the protection of the white courts which they discreetly avoided.

Two court cases brought against the agency illustrate the dichotomy in the black and white cultures as they encountered each other in the courtroom. The cases were instigated by two sets of grandparents, one white and one black, for the repossession of their grandchildren placed in adoption without their knowledge. A white judge heard the case of the black grandparents and a black judge heard the case of the white grandparents. Both sets of birth parents were of age, of right mind, and had signed relinquishments of parental rights voluntarily and without duress.

The white mother, pressured into marriage by her parents to give her child legitimacy, was divorced soon after his birth. She kept her baby, living at home until she finished high school. Her parents then expected her to support her child and make her own way. She moved out and began the struggle, which continued for two years.

Transporting her son daily to and from the day care center, struggling to hold her lowly job, paying for child care, food, and the rent of a meager apartment, the mother believed she and her son would never emerge from the endless burden of their lives. She was troubled by her son's unhappiness, the limits of his experience, the restrictions on her own life. She was worried by increasing debt. She viewed her parents as neglectful and destructive, as illustrated by her own poor preparation to handle her life. She saw her younger sisters growing up under the same parental cloud. She was determined to save her son. After months of considered thought and with the cooperation of the birth father, the mother relinquished her son for adoption, convinced that only incorporation into a happy, wholesome family would save him from a grim life like her own. Months later, the grandparents became aware of their daughter's action and brought suit.

Two days into the trial, the black judge spoke from the bench commenting that his grandparents had raised him and twelve other grandchildren, thus disclosing the cultural heritage which inclined him toward the merits of grandparenthood. Against the protests of the mother, the adopters and the agency, legal niceties were ignored and the child was routed through the vascillating father back to the grandparents.

In the other case, the expectant black mother had come from the Midwest to a maternity home in Washington to have her baby adopted. The purpose of adoption was to save the reputation of her fiancee, a young minister, and to insure the mother's eventual partnership in an auspicious marriage to him. The plan was jointly agreed upon by the girl, her mother, and her fiancee, but not by her father, who knew nothing of her pregnancy.

The pregnancy and birth progressed normally. Adoption continued to be the chosen plan, despite the unexpected marriage of the fiancé to another woman. The baby was surrendered and placed in an adoptive home.

Several months later, the abashed mother and her own patriarchal grandfather appeared at the office to plead for the return of the baby. The baby's incensed grandfather had only within the week found out about his daughter's secret pregnancy and the adoption of his grandson. He dispatched his daughter and his ancient father to take possession of his grandchild, no matter what the cost.

The mother's apathetic acceptance of the plans of her male forebears was in distinct contrast to the uncomprehending and earnest distress of her grandfather. Never in the history of his family had such a debasing, inhuman act as adoption been perpetrated. My heart went out to him. If only they had come months before. But now it was too late. The adoption of six months must be protected.

The old man appealed to the agency with a gift of money, the only measure of worth he felt we would value. Explaining the protections of adoption provided under the law, I pointed out that only through action of the court could adoption be set aside. The mother, coerced by her father and grandfather, brought suit.

Several months later the trial was held. The mother came alone. She was represented by an inept lawyer who had no legitimate case. In opposition to these two downcast individuals was an array of white power: an imposing judge, the maternity home's case worker, director and lawyer, the adoption agency's director and attorney, and witnesses to the signing of the original documents of surrender.

The black birth father had come from the midwest with his new wife in defense of the agency, to add evidence to the fact that every legal technicality, every social service, every opportunity for the exercise of her free will had been afforded the mother. The agencies' records, the testimony of the witnesses and the legal papers demonstrated a thorough and tight case against deception and fraud, the only basis for setting aside the adoption.

The mother's lawyer, defeated even before he entered the court room, made one searing statement: "There are plenty of black babies out there nobody wants. Why can't you give the adopting parents one of them."

The irony of the situation was clear. The white experts regarded the legal aspects of the case with sanctity. The black participants saw the dilemma on a purely human level. Even before the case was tried, the black adoptive mother, on hearing of the suit, hugged her baby to her and said, "Your mother wants you back. Poor thing. I am sorry for her." After the trial, the birth father and his new wife turned to the defeated mother and offered to take her along on their long drive home. The puzzled mother wondered how her little black boy whom she simply wanted back had brought such monumental opposition from all those white people.

Although some of my examples of grandparental interferences picture tough and insensitive individuals, most grandparents were convinced that their daughters alone must make the choice between keeping their babies or placing them in adoption. Some, in expectation of the loss of their grandchildren, came to my office to see and talk with me, the person who would be responsible for the choice of adoptive homes. Hopefully the meetings brought reassurance and comfort to them.

Some grandmothers suffered such poignant sorrow at the loss of grandchildren that they appeared closer to the children than did the mothers themselves. In the agency we called them the "unmarried grandmothers". They, unlike their youthful daughters, were sensitive to the family bond and the continuity of the human chain from one generation to the other. They were the grandmothers who made inquiries of the agency about the babies' progress in the adoptive homes, who telephoned on birthdays, and who sent anonymous contributions to the agency.

One grandmother, after losing her daughter in an accident, called to ask the agency to let her grandson, growing up in an adoptive home, know about his mother's death. Her feeling of kinship to her blood grandchild was not lessened by the separation of fifteen years. Unable to have participated in the plans for his adoption, she had never relinquished her grandson. He was still her next of kin.

6 FOSTER MOTHERS

APPROACHING THE SUBURBAN home of Mr. and Mrs. Hanson, one imagined a prim conventional couple living there. The hedge and walk were neatly trimmed and the white clapboard house freshly painted. Only as one went into the backyard and saw a fluttering wall of dazzling diapers did one suspect that something unusual was going on inside.

Entering the Hanson's home, one was struck by the quiet, comfortable atmosphere and the utter cleanliness of the place. The smell of baking bread gave one the sense of a real old fashioned home.

On further inspection one came upon four bassinets in the corners of the dining room. Four tiny babies were asleep in them. There was no odor of soiled diapers, no sound of crying, and no confusion. In the kitchen, boiled and waiting, were innumerable nipples, soft and hard, with large and small holes adaptable to the sucking energy of each infant. Twenty-four six ounce bottles of milk stood ready. Far from fitting the conforming mold, the Hansons had chosen an unusual profession. They were foster parents to newborn infants.

Mrs. Hanson had become a foster mother by happenstance. She began one year by taking a neighbor's baby for several weeks and in the following twenty-five years became a mainstay of two adoption agencies. Not a hospital nurse or a day-time baby sitter, she was a twenty-four hour a day foster mother. She cared for 559 infants in her house-bound career.

One looked for the elaborate equipment of the modern nursery, the powders, the salves, the bottles, the pins, the bassinet, the pails, the bags and the baskets. There was none of this, only a high pile of clean and carefully folded diapers on one of the dining room chairs.

Their care reduced to basic simplicity, infants were bathed in the washbasin and dried on their mother's lap.

Over a period of twenty years I came to know Mrs. Hanson very well and was continually astonished at her talent for warm motherliness combined with her objective professionalism.

One day she said to me, "Watch this, it is an interesting phenomenon." A baby sucking peacefully and rhythmically on his bottle was turned over on his other side and shortly began sputtering and choking. "It is strange," she said, "but the babies nurse better on their left sides and about half of them will have difficulty nursing on their right." Mrs. Hanson confided that she was always reluctant to mention this observation to anyone for she had been scoffed at for the crazy notion. But one day her observation was confirmed by a visitor from Greece, the head nurse of Metera, a prominent Greek orphanage and adoption agency. The two "mothers" compared experiences with an enthusiasm that spanned cultural and language barriers. Mrs. Hanson asked, "Have you noticed that an infant nurses better lying on his left side?" "Yes, yes, of course. I do know that is true. I have seen it many times," the other replied.

The babies taught her about themselves and she became an authority on infant behavior whom the pediatricians, social workers, and adoptive parents turned to for elucidation.

Mrs. Hanson was often the one to alert the pediatrician to potential problems—the detached autistic child, the infant whose chin must be held up for sucking, the whimpering retarded child, the brain damaged spastic, the mongoloid, the cretin. She also found the lesser problems—the hernias, and the dislocated hips. She became a sort of sage, her observations never disregarded by either the pediatrician or the director of the agency.

Mrs. Hanson had only one problem. She couldn't keep babies more than six weeks without becoming so attached to them that their departure was a painful loss to her. The only compensation was to begin again with another three-day-old infant. When babies lingered longer than three months (there were situations that made delay necessary), I anticipated a difficult separation for her.

I will not soon forget the trauma of taking away a toddler Mrs. Hanson had had for over a year. I telephoned to let her know when I would arrive. I came to her door and rang the bell. I waited outside. A moment later she partially opened the door and handed the little boy to me. No word was spoken. No sympathy expressed. As I turned away I heard the proud and reserved Mrs. Hanson burst into tears. The very heart which made her such a superb foster mother also brought her unmitigated grief.

— — — — — — — — — —

Foster homes are the modern repository for children of broken homes and neglectful parents. They have taken the place of the orphanages of past generations. Social workers like to think of foster care as being temporary until children can be reunited with their families or other permanent plans can be made. But all problems do not lend themselves to quick and easy solutions, for children may be irreconcilable runaways, delinquent exhibitionists or retarded misfits. These children are sometimes placed with foster families unable to cope with the problems they present. In our planning for children we have swung full circle away from the imperfect institutional situation to the inadequate nuclear family.

Adoption appears to be a logical answer for dependent children waiting in foster homes for homes of their own. But if they are too old, or if their parents show even passing interest in them, the courts will not release these "children who wait" for adoption. Groups of concerned parents are working through the Council of Adoptable Children in the United States and The Open Door Society in Canada to pressure the courts and social agencies to more constructive action.

Delays are usual in the field of child welfare. The crises get the attention from the overburdened social workers and the days pass by for the quiet waiting children until they are too old to adapt themselves to change. Some of the older children and many of those in minority groups are eventually adopted by their foster parents who receive subsidies to help pay for their care. Even if children have lived all their lives in one foster home, they still sense the change to permanence which Subsidized Adoption gives them.

It is the problems of temporariness which makes care of children in foster homes so onerous and the reputation of foster mothers so poor. Foster mothers are separated from each other, they are unorganized and they have no public spokesman. Their low pay is increasing but, like all home jobs, the value of the work in monetary terms is hard to gauge. I once figured that a foster mother working twenty-four hours a day in infant care was receiving twenty-one cents an hour. It was thought that if they received more they might work for money instead of for love.

Thirty years ago children used to be purposely moved from one foster home to another. It was thought injurious for children to become too attached to one foster mother, because the adjustment to another or to their parents would be harder and it was feared a subsequent adoption might not work out at all. Now we are upset by the number of changes children make from one foster home to another. There are not enough good foster families for all the children who need them, and there can be no final commitment in a system of child care which is temporary. Old time orphanages, if impersonal, were at least permanent.

I recall an adoptive father who grew up in the orphanage for boys in Hershey, Pennsylvania and felt such attachment to the place that he considered it his home and returned for frequent nostalgic visits.

Foster homes are a mainstay of the adoption agencies. They provide the maternal care a newborn baby needs and give the birth parents time to choose the best course of action.

I recall one foster mother who took a young unmarried couple into her home with their week-old baby so that they could make their plans. They decided to get married and keep their son. It was a hasty wedding, a friendless ceremony and I was the only witness. The scared and uncertain newlyweds, let down by the undecorous ceremony, returned cheerless to the foster home. They were greeted by the foster mother who had cooked and decorated a many-tiered wedding cake for them. Their spirits rose. As we sat at the kitchen table drinking coffee and eating the cake the bridegroom rocked his baby and we celebrated.

In most agencies, the foster mothers are out of the main stream in the adoption procedures. The agencies do not grant the foster mothers the kind of trust that would make them members of the team. Agencies fear breach of confidentiality by the foster parents, and, through elaborate and complicated ruses, often set up a system with two sets of names for each child, giving the alias to the foster families.

Perhaps social workers, in their struggle to be uniquely professional, have constructed a wall around themselves to shut out the non-professional foster mothers. It would make more sense to screen the foster parents with greater care to begin with, to insure their trustworthiness, and then to use their talents as observers and consultants on infant and child development. Considering that foster parents frequently adopt their foster children, it is only sensible to make a thorough investigation in the first place.

Foster mothers have cared for the sick and the handicapped, the unadoptable as well as those adopted. Those I have known have had to deal with epileptic seizures, meningitis, heart failure and crib death. They have had to recognize and act upon emergency situations, such as pyloric stenosis, hydrocephalus and hernia, all of which required immediate surgery. Any mother faced with even one of these problems might be overwhelmed. Yet the foster mothers I have known have carried these burdens with intelligence and good will.

Two of the foster families with whom I worked adopted their foster children. One, a little girl, petted and adored since birth, was adopted at age three despite occasional epileptic seizures which terrified her parents. Tragically, only two months after the family celebrated her adoption, she died of the brain damage she had suffered at birth. The other child, a boy, was hydrocephalic. He was operated upon at a few weeks of age and given a chance of life with the insertion of a shunt valve in the side of his head to carry off the accumulated fluid under his skull. The prognosis was poor and there were no adopters. Miraculously, his condition was stabilized and he was adopted at age four by the only family he had ever known, his foster family.

Children already relinquished by their birth mothers often remain too long in their foster homes because of inexcusable delays. Some agencies wait until the children are relinquished and only then begin to study possible adoptive homes. Children wait for social workers to make appointments with doctors, to complete paper work, to organize placement conferences, and to submit the papers to the court.

In my practice, foster mothers were members of the staff, their homes available to both parents and adoptive parents. An unmarried mother, torn by indecision, could visit her baby and the person who cared for him in the place where he lived. Adoptive parents who wished to see the child before they proceeded with adoption could also visit him in his foster home. The foster mother who had grown to love the baby was reassured to see how much the new parents appreciated the baby, and received special thanks from them for getting the baby off to a good start. Furthermore, the foster mother was able to ease adopters into their parental tasks by sharing with them the ways of their new charge.

To be sure that the paths of the adoptive and birth parents did not cross, we needed only to be good traffic managers. They never did cross and I have never known a foster mother who did not honor her pledge of confidentiality.

Parents sometimes return to show the foster mothers what marvelous children the babies have become, and the children accompanying them see the house where they first lived and the woman who cared for them. These visits are a reassuring touch with the past for many adoptees.

Agency foster mothers hesitated at first to take black babies into their white homes. It wasn't the babies that bothered them, it was the neighbors. In one all-white neighborhood a black foster baby began the integration of the street. It happened this way.

A racially-prejudiced white family lived next door to one of the agency's foster homes. The neighbor woman was curious when the foster mother spoke of caring for a dark skinned "Spanish" baby but thought little of it. However, one day, when returning some borrowed sugar to the foster mother, she was astounded to see the foster mother holding and kissing the cheeks of a black infant.

"Why that baby is a Negro," she declared in horror. "Yes, he does seem to be black," replied the foster mother, "and isn't he darling." She continued to cuddle the baby, talking to him as the neighbor watched. Finally the neighbor could not resist and asked to hold him. She praised his straight back, his soft hair and the way he held his head up so strongly for one so young.

But as she left, she fell back into her biased pattern. She said, "Of course all babies are cute. It's just when they grow up they change."

A few days later a black adoptive couple came to the foster home to see the baby for the first time, but the baby and the foster mother had been delayed at the doctor's office. They were not at home.

It was snowing. The couple stood outside while the neighbor watched from her kitchen window. Finally overcoming her instinctive resistance, she invited them in from the cold. She gave the couple hot coffee and sat with them in the kitchen while they waited for the baby's return. The neighbor felt the excitement of the adopting couple and was caught up in their anticipation.

The next day she went to the foster home to tell the foster mother of her amazing discovery. "You wouldn't believe it. They were such really nice people, so refined and polite, and such nice manners. They thanked me for being so kind. I've never met anyone like them before."

She picked up the baby and this time *she* kissed him on the cheek, telling him, "Are you ever lucky!"

7 ADOPTED: THE CHILD LEARNS THE WORD

JANE AND HER MOTHER WERE at the grocery store. Mrs. Thayer, placing melons in her shopping basket, was preoccupied with selecting the fruit when out of the blue her three-year-old daughter asked, "Why is Aunt Mabel so fat in the stomach?" Most mothers, even if they did not find the setting exactly fitting, would be amused and proceed to explain that a baby was growing inside Aunt Mabel.

But this was the moment Mrs. Thayer had anticipated with such dread. For Mrs. Thayer was an adoptive mother. She knew that there was more involved than a simple statement could cover, and she could not face the question until she could weigh her thoughts and her words in a quiet setting. "We'll wait until we get home and then I'll tell you." When they got home Jane had forgotten all about her question, but Mrs. Thayer had not. She talked it over with her husband. He suggested letting the matter pass. "Don't worry, she's not anxious so why should you be?" But Mrs. Thayer could not put it out of her mind, and at the end of each day she wondered if she should bring up the subject or wait for Jane to ask the question again.

Fortunately Aunt Mabel delivered the baby soon afterward, presenting the opportunity to explain to Jane where babies come from.

"Do you remember when you asked me what made Aunt Mabel so fat? Well, she was big because the baby was living inside her. When he was born he came outside and now you can see him."

"Was I born like that? Was I inside your tummy?"

"No, you were born from another lady's tummy." Before further questions were asked, Mrs. Thayer was propelled by her anxiety into an explanation.

"You see, you were adopted. Babies come two ways, some like Aunt Mabel's and some by adoption."

She had rehearsed what she planned to say but it didn't come out the same. Mostly she wanted to reassure Jane, who, she assumed, must be going through an emotional trauma equal to her own. She had heard that adopted children feel rejected by their birth mothers. She wouldn't want Jane to feel rejected. She was way ahead of three-year-old Jane.

"We couldn't have any children," she continued, "and we wanted a little girl. We chose you. We love you just the same as if you were born to us."

There was a long pause, broken by Jane's observation, "I guess I was in the wrong tummy."

Jane's mother and father prided themselves on having fulfilled their obligation to tell Jane she was adopted. They decided not to discuss adoption further in front of her and thereby put the subject to rest. Mrs. Thayer was confident that she had handled the question satisfactorily since Jane continued to be an untroubled and happy child. Looking back, she found the ordeal not as difficult as she had imagined and, looking forward, she was sure that a smiling and much loved child like Jane would not speculate about her adoption further. She was convinced that disclosure at an early age had ended Jane's concern.

— — — — — — — — — —

At one time in the lives of most of us, we believe we may have been adopted. It comes when we feel sorry for ourselves, think we are ignored and unappreciated by our parents. The feeling is one of loneliness and abandonment. In a moment of conflict with our parents, the notion of another mother and father may provide a romantic sense of self-justification. This is the background upon which our social orientation to adoption is founded. Adoptive parents have to face this deep-seated attitude when they undertake to raise adopted children with the same security and acceptance as birth children.

"Adopted" is an emotional word stirring up reactions from the depths of the unconscious. Words associated with adoption are generally negative: orphan, foundling, bastard, illegitimate, wayward, unwanted. No wonder adoptive parents are so sensitive, so reluctant to tell their children, and so fearful that they will be casting them into baneful molds by labeling them with the word "adopted." Couples who adopt children are presented with special problems and unusual challenges in bringing their children through to adulthood with self-confident wholeness.

Most of the time adoptive parents think little about adoption. They are busy in the day-to-day job of giving, demanding and responding to their children. During their first child's infancy, parents forget adoption altogether and bask in the reality of their long-held dream of having a baby to love and care for. What a relief it is when they can put behind them their preoccupation with the adoption process, medical treatment for infertility, interviews for the social investigation, legal consultations, court procedures, and endless waiting. It is remarkable how one seven-pound gurgling infant can kick away old frustrations, and turn a house for living into a home with a future. No wonder a first child holds a special place for adopters. As one mother said, "My first child mended my broken heart."

For several years adoption and its uncertainties can be ignored, even put out of mind altogether. One mother recalled, "I forgot he wasn't born to me. When my friends talked to me about their deliveries, I was startled to realize that I hadn't borne my son after all." An adoptive mother, after years of longing for a child, can blind herself to the fact of his adoption when she takes her first infant to her heart as her own. Even without the nine months of gestation, which so mysteriously cements the newborn to his birth mother, the adopting mother has the same strong maternal feeling for her child. It is this phenomenon which makes adoption a positive life experience and the adoptive family a true family from the beginning.

As the child moves into his third or fourth year, parents become increasingly apprehensive about how and when to tell him he was adopted. The care-free days of his infancy are passing, and the parents are faced with the uncertainty common to all adopters.

Revealing his adoption to a child is more traumatic for the parent than for the child. What to a young child may be merely a new word, an odd event, is for the parent a significant step into the unknown. In her mind the mother is letting her child down in revealing that he was not hers by birth but, in reality, born to another. It is a confession of regret for the parent, and for the child an introduction to an endless mystery. The revelation represents a premature separation of child and parent occurring long before the normal time of a child's independence from his parents. The confession of adoption is a moment of truth that few adopters forget. In fact, so strongly are the circumstances, place and time rooted in the parents' memory that all the mothers I talked to could recall every detail of those moments.

One wonders how parents summon the nerve to tell their children they are adopted, so strongly must their protective instincts inhibit them from doing so. But usually they follow the advice of the social worker, telling children of their adoption by the time they are five before they enter school.

Some overzealous parents begin saying the word "adoption" to their babies while they are infants in their arms. They reason that a baby should get used to hearing the word. But making "adoption" a common household word is more likely to condition the parents than the child. There is danger in overemphasizing the word. Adoption may become such a habit of speech that the child will never escape the singular designation.

Some parents combine pleasant adjectives with "adopted" to give adoption a happy rather than a forbidding connotation. They refer to "our darling adopted son" or "our sweet adopted daughter." It is as if the good adjectives, "darling" and "sweet" would cancel out the bad one, "adopted."

Children are apt to take the word in stride when it is spoken openly and without emotion. A candid approach by the parents results in a matter-of-fact reaction by the child. One little girl of seven, when asked by her mother, "And how is my little adopted bunny today?" ignored the word "adopted" and answered in disgust, "I'm not a bunny."

After the period of their children's early years, most parents are reluctant to dwell on adoption. They do not want to think of themselves as different from other parents, nor do they wish to consign their children to this minority group. Many parents enjoy having strangers note resemblances between them and their children, since the presumption of blood ties gives them such a pleasurable sensation. However, the privilege of privacy in family matters cannot be contained when children confide to special friends the deep secret of adoption or boast about being chosen.

The "chosen child" has become a romantic unreality in modern times, when the choice is, in reality, made by the social agency or the doctor, not by the parents. Furthermore it puts the birth child, who "had to be taken," in a curious position. The adopted and birth child need not be compared. The fact that they sometimes are merely demonstrates that adopters are trying to make up to their chosen children for the deep-seated feeling that adoption is second best. It is as if the adopted child requires an extra dimension of love to equal what other children already have. Although adopted children have problems unique to them, being unloved by their parents does not seem to be one of them. In families with both adopted and birth children, I have observed no preference based on origin.

There is general acceptance that early revelation of adoption is wise. It is based on the unfortunate experiences of adoptees who found out late in adulthood that they were adopted. Parents realize that it is virtually impossible to keep the secret in these days of documentation, of active social agencies, of knowing friends and curious relatives. One parent said, "The children have to know. It can't be helped. Adoption is their cross to bear."

I found only one family where the children, seven and nine, were unaware, as far as the parents knew, that they were adopted. The mother felt they should be told, but the time had never seemed right. She was fearful of hurting them. In her uncertainty, she doubted that if they knew they would feel the same toward her.

Parents are convinced that their children should first hear about adoption from them. Yet in many families, hesitation in telling may result in the children learning about their adoption from others in most unfortunate ways. Instead of the door being opened to further questions, a shadow descends again over the touchy subject.

Sensitivity to parents' feelings, manifest in most children, is especially marked in adopted children. If parents seem uncomfortable in talking about adoption, young adoptees seeking parental approval keep questions to themselves. The fact that children do not question does not necessarily mean they are not thinking about adoption.

Most adoptive parents wait for their children to introduce the subject. At the age of three or four, children begin to observe the outside world and ask such questions as "Why is that lady so fat?" "Where did Aunt Grace get her baby?" or "How did Princess get all those puppies?" It is usually the adoptive mother, who is with the child most of the time, who is confronted with the inevitable disclosure which these questions pose. "Babies and puppies come out of their mother's tummies," a mother may explain. The child, in logical sequence then asks, "Did I come out of your tummy?" This is the moment all mothers remember, the moment when the other woman invades the intimate union of mother and child.

Once a mother has told her child he was adopted, she is relieved and finds that the much-dreaded task was not so difficult after all. She reaches out to her child in sympathy. Projecting her own assumption that he had been rejected, she wishes to compensate with all the reassurance possible. While the child may be trying to figure out how he came out of some lady's stomach, his mother may be explaining over and over that he was special and had been chosen.

The second, third and subsequent children in a family do not pose the same trial for the parents. The ice was broken with the first and, child though the facts may have to be repeated, the younger children are always aware of adoption through its common knowledge in the family. Often the first child joins the parents in the adoption of the second, making the trip to the agency to pick up the new baby. These apparently harmless journeys are sometimes baffling for young adoptees between the ages of two and five, who are old enough to sense that babies come from somewhere but not old enough to comprehend the adoption process.

One little girl of four had been told that there were two ways to get babies, one by birth and one by adoption. As she stood over the bassinet in the agency waiting room, she stared down at her baby brother and thoughtfully commented, "You weren't born either."

The picture of growing in another woman's stomach must seem a ridiculous notion to a small child, for the four-year olds usually do not pursue the subject. They need time to absorb the meaning of the strange facts of their births before the next successive thoughts come to their minds.

The relationship of a fat stomach to pregnancy and birth is particularly vivid in the minds of older adopted children, since they have to picture not only one but two tummies in the complicated explanation of adoption. The seven-year-old son of a lawyer said, "There ought to be a law that you should come out of your own mother's tummy." Another incensed young boy resented the confusion between his two mothers and protested angrily to his adoptive mother, "Why didn't I grow in your stomach like other kids around here?"

The role of the social worker, although clear to adopters, is not grasped by their children. Adopted children cannot place the fabled social worker in any world they know of. They may be confused and somewhat threatened by her part in their lives. A visit by her stimulates questions which reveal misapprehensions lying dormant in the minds of puzzled adopted children. A mother's glowing introduction of the social worker as "the lady who brought you to us" can raise the specter in the child's mind of the birth mother herself.

In one harrowing experience I was met at the door by an excited girl of six who looked at me expectantly and asked, "Are you my mother?" She was crushed by my denial, her mother was anguished by the question and I was at a loss to find a way to make it up to her for not being the one she wanted me to be. Later I found that her conscientious mother had carefully explained that some children are born and some come from the social worker.

Confusion is compounded by parents speaking of the social worker as "Granny" or "our grandmother". Flattering as it is to the worker to be thus drawn into the family orbit, the logical question that occurs to the child will be, "So where is my mother?"

"The woman who gave you to us" can also be, in the child's mind, "the woman who can take you away." The authority to remove, like the ability to present, is linked with the all powerful social worker. Unfortunately some parents play on this fear and, either in jest or in anger, threaten to call the agency to come and get their children.

In one poignant visit I made to an adoptive family, the older child, a girl of eight, attempted to divert my attention from her baby brother by aggressive and aggravating behavior. She feared I had come to take him away.

It is different when a child is adopted at the age of four or older. He has a memory of the past and knows, or at least hopes, that he is being adopted. The parents need not destroy an illusion of his being their birth child. They can start from where they found him, with honesty about his past life, so difficult to come to terms with in infant adoption.

One would think that black or *Oriental* children in white homes would take adoption for granted because of their obvious dissimilarity to the parents. But until adoption is explained, they may be especially troubled. Instead of feeling strange when their adoptions are explained they are often relieved to understand why they appear so different from their parents.

Once children are told of their adoption their parents can tell them how it took place. The stories renew happy memories for parents and convey to the children a feeling of love and warmth.

The often repeated tale is of a couple who wanted a baby and couldn't have one themselves. They prayed and waited and finally saw the little girl they had always longed for. They knew she was theirs right away. The story goes on with details of taking her home, the joy, the pride, the disbelief that such a beautiful baby was theirs. One boy was told that he cried when he first saw his parents. His explanation later as an eight-year-old was, "I must have cried when I first saw you because I was so glad to be coming home to this house."

I will always remember the recounting of adoption by a master storyteller who enthralled me with the verbatim account as she had told it to her daughter. She carried the tale in utter suspense from the beginning, when the Lord led the parents to the adoption agency and the social worker told them about a baby waiting for them, right to the door of the foster home.

"We walked up the front steps. I was shaking all over like a puppy after a bath, and your father was very quiet. But his face looked like a ripe tomato so I knew he felt just the way I did. Knock, knock, knock! We wanted to go inside. No answer. Knock, knock, knock! Still there was no answer. Do you think our baby has flown away? She can't even walk yet. Let's try again. Knock, knock, knock! The door opened and there was a nice lady who said, 'You've come to see your baby.' But we couldn't find you anywhere. We looked in the hallway, no baby; then we looked in the living room, still no baby. We peeked in the kitchen. No baby there. Suddenly we spied a little basket in the corner of the dining room. It looked like my laundry basket, but it had a pink flounce around it. We crept over on tiptoes because we were sure you must be in it. But there was no baby to be seen, just a humpy pink blanket. I thought it must be the laundry after all. 'Where do you suppose she is,' we wondered. Well, you were there all the time. The nice lady lifted back the humpy blanket and there was a little pink baby all curled up in a heap. Do you know who that baby was? That baby was you. You looked so sweet and happy that we named you Joy."

The need to recreate the circumstances of adoption into a tale of happy adventure is almost universal with adopters. They seek to convey their special pleasure and dispell any doubts their children may have that adoption is peculiar or mysterious. Some parents read books to their children, such as *The Chosen Child,* about a fictitious adoptee and his parents. Others, more imaginatively, tell their own stories.

One parent told the story in the third person, and even when the child knew the story well he kept up the pretense of its novelty as a game. At the end of the tale, when his mother asked, "And what do you think that little baby's name was?" He would shout with joy, "John Ross, that's me!"

Another mother wrote the story of adoption for her two children and put it into book form, so that after the years of having it read aloud to them they could peruse it for themselves. The cover was well worn by frequent rereadings.

When there are several children in the family, the individual tales are easy to confuse. One mother resolved this problem by making a composite birth story for her four children, but making the differences in a unique way. By saving the four baby outfits which the children wore when they came home as infants, she showed their homecomings to have been memorable events, distinct one from another. The girls in the family loved to get out their bonnets, dresses and baby blankets and to imagine themselves small enough to wear such tiny garments.

Just as children love the story of adoption, they love the pictures and movies taken on the day of adoption. Sometimes these pictures are put in baby books, with birth weight and length, growth and development, and all the rest of the early medical and social history. Some parents, very pleased and at home with adoption, have used *My Adoption Baby Book* to record the early months. Later on these books may for a time be cast aside by the growing adoptees, as self-consciousness about being adopted prompts them to secrete so blatant a revelation from their friends.

One family spoke of themselves as "an adopting family." First the father and mother adopted each other. Then they adopted their oldest child. A few years later all three adopted the second child, and then they all four adopted the cat and dog. Another less playful family was incensed with this idea, saying, "It is wrong to put animals in the same category as children."

The day of adoption is a very important anniversary for adopting parents, and some parents acknowledge this by celebrating the day each year with a party. For a family who adopted three siblings, aged three, four and six, at the same time, the adoption day was an appropriate anniversary because the children remembered it as a special day too. But in most adoptions there is danger that in emphasizing the adoption day parents are belittling the day that is significant for the child, the day of his birth. To adoptive parents, the baby's life started the day he came home to them, and the early weeks or months as well as the day of his birth did not belong to them. One mother had to be reminded by her perceptive husband to speak of "the year Billy was born" instead of "the year we got Billy."

8

QUESTIONS CHILDREN ASK

JANE AT FOUR HAD BEEN TOLD that babies come from inside their mothers. She was told that she did not come from her own mother but from inside another woman. Her parents had emphasized that Jane was special having been chosen and adopted. Although Jane's parents did not speak of adoption after the one conversation they assumed that Jane remembered.

However, when Jane was seven she astounded her mother by asking. "What does adoption mean? Bobby said I was adopted."

"Don't you remember? I told you about being born from another lady and then we adopted you. Don't you remember how I explained you were special, that you were chosen?"

Jane was puzzled and thoughtful. "I don't remember. I didn't know I was adopted. This lady who had me in her tummy, who is she?"

Jane's mother said she didn't know and protested ignorance to all questions that followed. "Did you see her?" "What did she look like?" "Where did she live?" "Do you know where she is now?"

Much to her mother's relief Jane stopped asking questions about her birth mother and turned to questions about herself; "Where was I born?" "Was I cute?" "How much did I weigh?" "Did you see me when I was little?" "How old was I when you got me?" Jane's mother felt comfortable about answering these questions, all but the last one, "Did I have a name when I was born?"

With renewed anxiety the mother explained to her daughter, "I don't know whether you had a name or not. It doesn't matter anyway because you have one now. It is a very nice name because it is your real name and we are your real mother and father."

— — — — — — — — — —

Not all children ask questions. Usually biological parents think little of it, believing that their children are just *that way*. But if the children are adopted, the parents are less casual. Most adopters expect their children to be curious and prepare themselves for questions about birth and birth parents. They may become perturbed and wonder if something is wrong when their children ask nothing. Some try to help their children express themselves by bringing up the subject of adoption to them. Others interpret the lack of questions as a sign that their children are not interested in their births or in their adoptions and are content and happy in their adoptive homes, just as if they had been born there.

But there is no doubt that adopted children think about their adoption more often than they verbalize their thoughts. They listen, observe and absorb the atmosphere in their homes as keenly as trained psychologists. They catch the tension and hesitation of their parents to certain questions. When an adopted child asks, "What did I look like when I was born?" he notices the response is different in tone from the response to, "Why do I have to eat spinach?" He may not be able to fathom why, but he soon learns that some questions upset his parents. The same questions an adoptee might avoid in childhood to save his mother pain he may use later as a rebellious adolescent to hurt her.

The initial responses parents make to questions about adoption are keys to future communications with their children. Negative replies to first questions may close the door to further ones, if children get the impression that the subject of adoption is somehow bad and not to be openly discussed. The children may take upon themselves the blame for their parents' displeasure, and feel ashamed for being adopted. The danger is that children so conditioned may never be comfortable in expressing themselves and will bottle up their thoughts about other sensitive subjects as well.

But parents alone do not create inhibitions in their children's questioning about adoption. The biases of society and the personalities of the children themselves play a part.

Most of the adoptive parents I interviewed were constructive and positive in answering their children's questions. Even so, the children did not necessarily pursue the subject with candor. Some adoptees, reserved and taciturn, asked no questions at all, though they were not discouraged from it by their parents. Others persisted in questioning with no apparent encouragement.

The questions were similar. Adoptees varied only in the number of questions they asked. Although it is difficult to generalize and dangerous to draw conclusions, I found a few provocative facts from my interviews with adoptive parents.

For example, the girls asked more questions than the boys. Only-children were universally persistent in their questioning, whereas in large families, some children demanded answers while others merely listened. The questioning seemed to have no relation to the socio-economic class of the adoptive families or to whether the families had birth children as well as adopted children.

One could speculate that girls, identifying with motherhood, were more curious about birth in general and their own in particular; that only-children had time for contemplation and the undivided attention of their parents for questioning; that in families of several children, those who asked no questions got answers to their non-verbalized thoughts through their siblings who did ask. The ease with which adopted children communicate with parents seems to depend not on social status, wealth, or education but on the emotional security of their fathers and mothers.

One might surmise that in an intellectually-oriented adoptive home where many issues are openly discussed adoption would be a natural subject of conversation between parents and children. But I found an atmosphere of open acceptance of adoption to be more vital than fluency. One mother who admitted difficulty in expressing her feelings about adoption transmitted such warm affection to her child that her daughter was able to articulate for her. Reading her mother's thoughts, she commented one day, "You know I don't look anything like you. Most girls seem to look like their mothers. Does it bother you that your little girl doesn't look at all like you?" It pleased the mother that her daughter understood her so well.

Within families of three or four children there is usually variation in the amount of interest in adoption expressed by the children. But I found that in several families all the children were equally curious and in others all equally silent on the subject of adoption. In three families none of the children questioned their parents, and in two all the children asked for detailed descriptions of themselves and their first parents. Was this uninformity just happenstance or was it an echo of their parents' position on adoption? I suspect the latter.

The usual situation is different, as illustrated by a family of five children, ranging in age from fifteen to seven. They were adopted at two-year intervals by average middle class parents.

The oldest, a boy, was a quick-tempered, athletic adolescent, pursued by girls but not yet interested in dating. Apparently indifferent to adoption, he asked few questions and remarked on hearing of my impending visit to his home. "I don't feel any different being adopted or not adopted. I'm not interested." The only time he mentioned his birth mother was to ask if she was a prostitute. The second child, another boy, was small in stature, quieter, and more sensitive than his older brother. He had asked more questions than any of the other children about himself, his birth, and especially his birth mother. He wanted to know what she looked like, if she was like him, but especially, "Why didn't she take care of me?" The third child, a girl, was a temperamental loner, an unhappy rebel, wanting approval yet making it difficult for others to give it. She had never asked questions about her birth parents, and only when her mother raised the matter did she say, "Why should I ask? You don't know the lady and anyway you are my real mother." The fourth child, a girl of nine, was a secure child, easy going, helpful and generous. She often forgot she was adopted and had expressed no interest in her birth parents. Once in a burst of enthusiasm, she had announced in her Sunday School class, "I'm eight years old. I'm adopted. I'm proud of it." The seven-year-old girl was the family pet, a bright, lively and talkative tomboy. She spoke freely about her birth mother, asking her age, her appearance, and what kind of person she was. Her mother explained, "She must have been a very nice lady to have such a nice girl as you." The daughter replied, "She couldn't have been very nice if she gave me away." Then she hugged her mother, "I want to be just like you Mommy, and adopt babies."

First questions are always about self, "Where was I born?", "How big was I?", "Was I cute?" The self-centered absorption of children is natural and does not often disturb their adoptive parents.

Many adoptees in my study, almost all of them boys, had not reached out beyond their self-interest to ask questions about their birth parents. But normally, as adoptees grow older, their curiosity about their birth mothers increases, and they begin a new line of questions: "What was her name?" "Did you ever see her?" "What did she look like?" Such questions reintroduce the specter of the rival mother whose position as birth parent threatens the maternal autonomy of the adoptive mother. Filled with her own anxieties, the mother fails to recognize that her children's early questions are without emotional content, motivated only by curiosity. For deeply buried in many adoptive mothers are the unresolved emotions of uncertainty, envy, and inferiority, based upon ther inability to conceive and to acknowledge the other parents who gave birth to their beloved children.

Some children who are aware of their parents' discomfort in talking of first mothers find ways of asking questions indirectly. One child of ten, feigning indifference to the subject, asked her parents certain facts about her adoption, because Aunt Sheila was curious and wanted to know.

As the years pass, adoptive mothers appear to lose their anxiety about the first mother as a rival and their fears of her prior claim to the children. In my study, I found that 58 percent of the parents of children under ten would discourage their children from a search for their birth mother, while only 28 percent of the parents of children over fifteen would react similarly.

For young adoptive mothers the designation of "mother" is not easily shared with birth mothers. Although in general usage the mother is the person who gives birth, in the adoption vocabulary the mother is the person who raises the child. A question innocently asked by a six-year-old, "What was my real mother like?", can unnerve an adoptive parent. She will explain, "Your real mother is the one who brings you up, who takes care of you and sees that you are well and happy. She is the one who loves you day after day and helps you grow up to be a good and responsible person." She may add as an afterthought, "Any woman can give birth," a sad protest from those women who experienced great personal ordeals in trying to do just that.

So parents teach their children other ways of referring to their female birth parent. The birth mother becomes "the woman who brought you into the world," "the lady who bore you," "the lady whose tummy you were in," "the other lady." Some children refer to their birth mothers as "she" or "her", an unspecified female object. Most children, assimilating their parents' sensitivity, avoid the term "first mother" or "other mother" unless the parents have already used the designation themselves. One child solved the dilemma of terminology by calling her adoptive parent her real mother, and her birth parent her pretend mother.

It is confusing for an adopted child to hear the term "real mother" used generally outside the family to mean the birth mother and have to remember to forget it in his own home. In some families in which the birth parent is spoken of as the first mother, the children are freer of this perplexity. One boy, born of one mother and in foster care of two others, was adopted at the age of six by still another. He blithely declared, "I like my fourth mother best," and felt her no less a mother for being the fourth.

I have never heard adopters speak of "the mother you don't know." Perhaps for the parents the expression conjures up the uncomfortable image of the mother you might know—someday.

It is interesting that adopted children rarely ask about their birth fathers. Young children envision their lives commencing at the moment of birth with the birth mother, for, only later when conception is understood, do birth fathers have any place in the adoptee's consciousness. Yet even during adolescence adopted young people seldom raise questions about their birth fathers. Only the boys wishing to identify with their male parent may ask, "Was he tall like me? Did he play football?"

Alert parents usually sense when their children are troubled. Odd or excessive behavior is as sure a clue as moodiness. One adoptive mother wondered what possessed her nine-year-old who had become quite unexpectedly a disciplinary problem. It never occurred to her that his adoption might be troubling him, as he was a child who asked so little on that subject. Then one day he blurted out, "You don't care about me. You're not my real mother. You didn't born me." Shocked by the intensity of his feelings, she pulled herself together and explained: "Of course I love you and so did your other mother, the one who bore you. We both love you, but she had you for only nine months and I have had you for nine years so you see I have loved you longer." Miraculously, the boy's behavior changed and his mother gained new insight into the profound emotions adoption creates and the simple means that can bring relief.

Some children seem too active, too busy, too occupied with other interests to give thought to adoption. One such boy, ten, the youngest of four adopted children, asked his dumbfounded mother one day, "Is it true I was adopted? Carl asked me in school today whether I was adopted like the rest of the family."

His incredulous mother said, "Of course, you know you are. What did you tell him?"

"I didn't remember, I don't listen to all that stuff everyone around here is always talking about. I just told him, "I don't know if I'm adopted or not. I'll go home and find out." His mother shook her head, wondering where this bright son of hers had been all his ten years.

Some early questions that seem of slight importance at the time they are asked may grow in significance later on. The questions "What was my name before?", "Did the lady who had me give me a name?", "What was my other mother's name?" are the first signs that the adopted child perceives himself as having been a person before he was adopted. This recognition of another self may smoulder until he feels himself pulled apart and disconnected, his life before adoption severed from the rest. The need to reestablish the early weeks of life and the separate identity they represent becomes an obsession for some adopted persons.

"What was my name?" is the question whose answer can link an adoptee to his birth, his first parents, his origin, his heritage, and to his very existence. The name is the symbol of his lost identity. Later on, the adoptee's satisfaction in knowing his original name is confounded by a new complication, a double identity. The birth name signifies his lost youth altered by adoption, and his adopted name is associated with his living experiences. The adoptee's view of himself thus becomes disjointed, his identity lying somewhere between his two selves. One psychiatrist of my acquaintance persuaded the adoption agency where he was consultant to share the first and last birth names of the children with their adoptive parents. He felt that knowing their original names was important to the development of the children's sense of self. I am sure he trusted the names would be shared with the adoptees as they grew up, but adopters, like the rest of us, are able to block out and forget that which they find uncomfortable to remember.

Although a few parents are incensed that their children's birth names are withheld from them by adoption agencies, most parents prefer not to know and shun a chance divulgence. Coming across their child's birth name in conversation with friends, in persons they meet, in newspaper stories, is unsettling for parents as they conjure up the possibility that they have stumbled upon a blood kin of their adopted child. They believe the child will be affected similarly, so, if they know the name, they resist sharing it with him.

In independent adoptions the name of the birth mother appears on the document of relinquishment, as she surrenders her child directly to the adopters themselves. Thus in private adoptions the name of the birth mother may be more readily accessible than in agency adoptions where the agency serves to separate birth parents and adopters.

Customarily, adoptees placed in infancy are given new names, often family names of the adopting couple. Children adopted at a later age more often retain their original first names. In adopting children from abroad, many parents, sensitive to the children's need to identify with their birth country or their race, give them names appropriate to their national origin.

One question which would appear of natural interest to adopted children is rarely asked of their parents, not even after they are grown. It is, "Why didn't you born me?" The question touches on a sensitive area for adoptive parents, their infertility. Most parents prefer to keep this knowledge to themselves. However one unusual mother had explained her medical problem to her garrulous daughter. Some days later she was amused to overhear a matter of fact explanation as retold to a bosom friend, "My mother had to adopt us because her pipes didn't work."

9

BEYOND THE HOME: FRIENDS, NEIGHBORS, SCHOOLS AND THE MEDIA

KATHY HAD A GOOD FEELING ABOUT being adopted. She and her two brothers knew that their mother and father were special. Unlike parents of many of their friends, theirs listened and talked to them as if they were grownups. When the subject of adoption was discussed their parents presented the facts without sentimentality or disparagement. Kathy and her brothers accepted their adoptions as matters of fact.

Kathy was gregarious and ebullient at an age when, returning from school, she would invariably pick up the phone to continue, with endless chatter, conversations with her girl friends. One day she came home angry and upset. She would speak to no one but went to her room where she remained secluded all afternoon. Emerging at dinner time she revealed what was troubling her.

"Daddy, what's wrong with adoption?" she asked her father. Her puzzled father wanted to know why she asked. She explained, "Jean got mad at me today. She called me names. She said 'You're fat, you're stupid and you're adopted.' "

"How did you answer her, Kathy?" asked her father. Kathy replied, "I said I was not adopted. I told her I was born in Mommy's tummy and if she didn't believe me she could go ask Mommy." In pride and self-defense Kathy had had to lie. It was her first exposure to what people outside her family thought about adoption. In one shocking moment she saw that being adopted was not good.

She could not explain to her father why she had lied. She just knew that she did not want to be an adopted girl any more. She wanted to be like her friends who were born into their families.

Several days later Kathy brought her friend, Jean, home for lunch. They had made up and were bosom pals again. Sitting at the table together, Kathy turned to Jean and said, "Now, you can ask Mommy." Jean, slightly embarrassed, then put the question, "Is

Kathy really an orphan?" Without hesitation her mother replied, "No, she has both a mother and a father, and they both love her."

Relieved and reassured, Kathy threw her arms around her mother and cried, "I have the best mommy in the whole world."

———————

An adoption is an event of unparalleled excitement in a neighborhood. The birth of a baby is taken in stride with a comment or two such as, "How many children does that make?" Yet the adoption of a baby inspires a flood of questions: "Where did you get her?" "Do you know anything about her?" "Is she illegitimate?" "Is it that hard to adopt?" "Can't you have your own?" "How do you have the nerve to take on someone else's child?" "How could any decent mother give up her baby?" "Are you going to tell her she's adopted?"

Added to the questions may be unsolicited comments: "All babies look alike." "They are so ugly when they are little." "You know, I think he looks just like your husband. What has he been up to?"

Neighbors who take for granted their right of inquiry about newly adopted children view the baby as an acquisition and the adoption as an arrangement, mysterious and intriguing, but without emotional content. How misguided they are. To the adopting couple, the baby is instantly a full-fledged member of the family and they are on the defensive to protect him.

One would think that as adoption became commonplace, witless questions would no longer be asked. But there are still "little old ladies" who ask in innocence, and curiosity seekers who inquire with insensitivity. One adoptive mother was asked, "You are so wonderful to have adopted all those poor homeless children. Do they call you 'Mother'?" Her reply must have taken the neighbor down a peg or two. She said, "They call me lots of things and one of them is 'Mother'."

Pity for the adopted child is almost universal. Without thought or knowledge, people refer to adopted children as "orphaned", "abandoned" and "unwanted." They may be romantically spoken of as "love children" in reference to their conception. Yet they become "unloved" when they are about to be adopted. A young observer, comparing the misfortunes of an adopted child who was ill said, "First she's adopted and now she's sick."

In defense of their children, adopters are apt to talk freely about their children's birth heritage as if to counteract the outsider's impression that adoptees are low class. Parents will regret later that, in their eagerness to put things right, they shared personal information which belongs only to the adoptee himself. Often when adopted children grow up they are incensed and angry that so many casual acquaintances seem to know so much about them, sometimes more than they themselves. Happy parents of newly adopted infants do not feign modesty when they boast about their babies' beauty and accomplishments. They admit that, at the beginning anyway, the credit goes to the birth parents and not to them.

Adoptive families that move frequently are often able to keep the fact of their children's adoptions from the neighbors. Secretive parents are relieved not to have to answer the same set questions which each new acquaintance would ask. Some parents experience quiet satisfaction in being considered just an ordinary family. But that joy may not last long, as their children, if they are young, will certainly spread the good word.

In the past an adopting mother might arrange admission to a hospital as if pregnant in order to receive, as her own, the baby of a mother who had just been delivered. In these days such an elaborate charade seems outlandish. Yet I knew one adopting mother who was so sensitive about her inability to have her own children that she pretended to have given birth to her adopted child. She padded herself as the months rolled along, stayed out of sight of the neighbors for several crucial days, and then came home with her "new born" baby in triumph. The fact that the baby was two months old and weighed about fourteen pounds spoiled her strategy.

Protected as they may be, adopted children soon learn that adoption means more than being chosen. They learn that adoption is a clandestine subject. An eight-year-old friend of Bobby's was told by his mother never to speak of Bobby's adoption to him. But the friend could not resist and one day he whispered to Bobby, "I know something about you but I can't tell you about it." Bobby became upset and anxious, troubled by uncertainties about himself. Was it about his adoption or was it something else? Had he done something wrong? Were people talking about him behind his back? Were his friends turning against him? He recalled the taunts of one of them, "So you're adopted. No one want you or something?"

Children also learn that adoption can be used as a weapon. Brad was not aware he was adopted. As an infant he had been placed with parents who seemed unable to conceive and was welcomed by them as their own. His adoption was downplayed and he was not told of it. When he was seven, his mother became pregnant, a fact also not shared with Brad. His closest playmate knew, however, and in a moment of anger he got back at Brad by striking at a defenseless area, his adoption. "You don't even know where babies come from. They come from their mothers' stomachs. But you didn't come from inside your mother 'cause you were adopted. You don't even know what adoption is. Adoption means your real mother didn't want you, so there. Did you know your mother is making a baby right now? It's in her stomach and when that baby is born she's not going to love you anymore."

They learn that adoption is bad. Sally met her friend at the corner on their way to school and as they walked along they talked. The friend asked, "How does it feel to be adopted?" Sally replied, "O. K. Like anything else."

Friend: "My mother thinks your mother never should have told you you were adopted."

Sally: "But there's nothing wrong with being adopted."

Friend: "Yes there is, my mother told me. She said your real mother and father weren't even married. And they didn't want you so they got rid of you."

Sally: "I don't care what you say. My mother told me they were nice and they wanted me to have the best home in the world."

Friend: "That's what she says but everybody knows that anyone who gives away her own baby is bad."

They learn that adoption is dramatic. Heather, Shirley, and Julie were best friends, all three imaginative in their play. The game they liked best was "orphanage", a game made real because eight-year-old Julie was adopted. Julie lent herself easily to a role as the abused and unloved orphan. Dominated by her older friends, she was flattered to be chosen for the central figure in the drama. They acted out all the woeful stories about orphans that they knew.

Sometimes Heather was the cruel stepmother, as in *Snow White,* or the witch in *Hansel and Gretel.* Heather especially enjoyed the role of the mean housewife turning Julie, the Little Match Girl, out into the snow. Reenacting fairy stories was fun, but one drama touched too closely to Julie's own experience.

Heather played the part of Julie's mother and Shirley became the proprietor of an orphanage. Taking Julie by the hand, Heather scolded her as they approached the orphanage. "I don't know what I'm going to do with you, Julie, you cry all the time. I haven't got any money to buy you a coat for winter and I don't have any food left to feed you either. I'll just have to put you in an orphanage."

Shirley met Heather and daughter Julie at the door of the orphanage. She let them in and, as the two "adults" discussed the situation, Julie listened. Heather, as the unmarried mother, confided in a clubwoman manner, "You know, of course, that Julie is illegitimate." Shirley, temporarily deserting her role as proprietor, asked, "What does that mean?"

The more sophisticated Heather explained. "Well you see Julie doesn't have a father. He went away to war and got shot. We were madly in love but we didn't have time to get married. I have to go back to work now so I'll leave Julie with you. Maybe you can find someone to adopt her." Turning to Julie she added, "Try to behave yourself and stop sniveling." Julie's pleasure in the game gave way to overwhelming anxiety as the drama seemed to become her own. She broke away and ran home.

Julie's tears and her mother's reassurances did not take care of the uncertainties the drama had aroused in her. But a week later her fears were allayed. She was playing alone in her room with her numerous dolls. "Raggedy Andy," she was heard to say, "Do you know that you are an orphan and you live in an orphanage? Do you know why? It is because you don't have any mother. That's very sad but we'll get you another mother. Raggedy Ann can be your new mother. Come, Raggedy Ann, and take Raggedy Andy out of the orphanage so he can go home."

What happens when adopted children go to school? Do the teachers know that they are adopted? Most teachers of the early grades usually seem to know. They learn it from parents, other pupils or from the students themselves. In some school systems there is a place on the student application to mark either "natural" or "adopted." Adoptive parents tend to resent the use of the designation "adopted" on an official paper. They feel the school's request for this information is an invasion of privacy and most would check the blank "natural" if confronted with the choice. They fear their children will be exposed to prejudicial and judgmental review of their behavior and scholarship because they are adopted.

However, teachers and counselors usually regard adoption information as germane and helpful in understanding the children. In knowing about their adoptions they think they will be able to protect adoptees from hurtful situations in the classroom. A mother who is eager to tell a sympathetic teacher about her child's adoption will resist letting a harsh teacher know. In all likelihood even if a parent wishes an adoption to be kept secret, the daily review of important events in "show and tell" will be an irresible opportunity for the first grader to unveil it himself.

Various stories were told me of experiences parents and children had had with teachers. One teacher, a neophyte psychologist, asked to be told the natural background of the adopted pupil. She felt she could assess her strengths and weaknesses and also know better what to expect of her. The adoptive mother was firm in refusing, saying, "That information is for my daughter alone. Besides the agency wouldn't approve."

A perceptive teacher was much touched by a thoughtful paper, written by an adopted pupil, called "My Adoption." She sensed it was too personal to share with the class but knew that the appreciation shown her parents in it would have great meaning for them. So instead of casting it away she saw that they got it.

Another teacher thought her rather dramatic pupil was lying when she declared she was adopted. The pupil, frustrated and angered by the teacher's disbelief, disrupted the classroom until confirmation of her adoption was received from home.

A teacher in a health class guilelessly deprecated adoption in her warning against out-of-wedlock pregnancies. Referring to adoption, she spoke of "unwanted" children. A bold ten-year-old did not take these observations in silence. She stood up before the class and said "I am adopted, and I'm glad I was born. And what's more I know my first mother cared about me. My mother told me so."

"My Autobiography" is a usual theme for social studies in the curriculum of fourth and fifth grade classes in both private and public schools. A good subject for most children, it can be perplexing for the adopted ones, as it magnifies the dilemma for them between true heritage and adopted heritage. For children who have not thought much about their natural background, the assignment forces them to face for the first time their double heritage.

Some adopted children ignore the assignment as if it did not apply to them. Others take on the heritage of their adoptive parents except for nationality or race. Most children, unresolved in their own minds, ask their parents how they should write the composition and, following their parents' advice, usually incorporate the adoptive ancestry as their own without mentioning adoption.

Newspapers and television play their part in provoking thoughts and raising questions in the minds of adopted children. Reporters for newspapers and writers of soap opera know that illegitimacy and adoption are sure-fire drama. Soap operas could hardly survive without out-of-wedlock pregnancies, rivalry between birth and adoptive mothers, and secret adoptions which everyone but the adoptee is aware of. If an adopted child gets into serious trouble, newspapers never fail to mention, as if by explanation, that he was adopted. The public reaction, I am afraid, is usually, "What do you expect?" Adopters, decrying the bad name which adoption is thus given, have protested to no avail.

Some parents are so discomforted by the way adoption is presented in the media that they throw away newspapers and turn off television when articles and programs depict adoption. For many the stories of adopted adults being reunited with birth parents are most disturbing of all. But parents cannot shield their children at all times or forever from exposure to adoption as the media present it. One evening, when their parents were absent, the young children in an adoptive family watched a program of "The Partridge Family." In it a child who thinks he is adopted goes from door to door searching for his first parents. It was a heart-rending show and the children reacted with fear, afraid that their first mother would come looking for them and would take them away.

A girl of eighteen, seeing a television program on adoptees in search of birth mothers, was cast down by the depiction of the mother turning her daughter away. When I talked to her about it, she expressed doubt that she would ever look for her mother now that she had seen the program. She had always imagined herself being welcomed in a reunion.

A young adopted boy, as a result of observing a log cabin delivery on a television western, answered a question he had wondered about for a long time. "Mom," he said, "now I know why you didn't have babies. It hurts too much."

Parents who try to shield their children from reading or hearing misleading and derogatory statements about adoption, or who dismiss prejudicial views as inconsequential might do better to follow the lead of an adoptive mother I spoke with. She pointed out to her children that being adopted set them apart as members of a minority group. She included herself, as an adoptive parent, in this group also. She explained that the majority of Americans did not try to understand those who were unlike them. She compared adoptive families to religious and racial minorities who had been misunderstood and scorned by the complacent majority.

She is convinced she can only strengthen adoption, not eliminate bias. She considers that being different is laudable. She encourages her children to value their adoptive family and to be proud in being adopted. She hopes they will reinforce each other as adopted siblings. She believes that if their views about adoption are positive and soundly based, prevailing prejudices will not be strong enough to overwhelm them. She trusts that their being adopted will not disorient the lives of her children.

10 ADOPTED CHILDREN IN ADOLESCENCE

BILL AND JOHN ARE BOTH 18. They were adopted into families as first children and were followed by the births of others. Both boys were born to educated couples and are intelligent and thoughtful young men. They are respected and loved by their adoptive parents. Both boys had been told in early years that they were adopted. At that point the similarities ceased. The reserved Bill and the tumultuous John moved poles apart in their apparent interest in adoption. The contrasting personalities of the boys, reinforced by the ease with which their parents spoke of adoption, brought about a striking dissimilarity. Bill is a conscientious and shy loner, who listens and observes the passing scene with stoic reserve. He had never asked any questions about his adoption. Finally when he was 14, his mother raised the subject herself, "You are getting older now, and I thought maybe we should talk about your adoption." He recalled having been told that he was adopted, but had let the knowledge rest there. Pressed by his mother for questions he might wish to ask, he said to his mother, "I don't have anything to ask. My family is here with you and Dad and Barbara. That's fine with me."

Bill's parents were concerned that he had asked nothing for now that he was grown they realized that they had so much to tell him.

John is a gregarious, volatile youth with a lively and imaginative eloquence. John had asked questions from early childhood. By the age of ten, his questions began to be emotionally charged, and by age 12, he was making bitter accusations. John's anger was directed at his birth mother, not his father. "I know they were not married, but that is no reason not to keep me. I was just thrown away like a piece of trash. If my mother couldn't care for me, why weren't there grandparents or aunts or someone who would take me?"

At 13, he transferred his hostility to his adoptive mother. "You're not my real mother, so you can't make me do that. Those grandparents aren't real either. You're just a fake mother." At 15, it was his identity that troubled him. "I'm going to change my name when I'm 21 and start fresh with a new name, not a fake name. I'm going to find my real mother. Just who am I really?"

And, finally, in concern for others like him, he said of an adopted neighbor child, "Poor kid, she'll never know who she is."

John's remarkable parents took it all in stride. His mother understood him well. She recognized his struggle with a growing ego and his need to save face with outlandish declarations. She believed "parents should create a climate that makes it possible for children to air feelings." His quiet and gentle father said, "It is fortunate to have had such an outspoken son, because I would have had a hard time bringing out the thoughts and feelings from a reserved child."

Will either boy really search for his birth mother? John with his fire and fury may have already cast the idea into the winds. Sensitive Bill who wouldn't want to hurt his parents may secretly strive to find her.

———————————

The emergence of self-centered interest and emotional turmoil, normal in adolescence, is more profound in the adopted person. His sexual preoccupation encompasses the mystery of his own conception and birth and creates a closer identity with his birth parents. As he speculates about their relationship, an adoptee may fabricate to his heart's content, for there are few facts to refute his fantasies as so little is usually known about his birth parents.

Adolescent fantasies seem to be of two extremes, either the birth mother (seldom father) was an actress and beautiful woman of the world, or she was a lowly street walker. It is unfortunate that adoptees, downgrading themselves, usually assume the latter. From early childhood they have picked up social attitudes which perceive parents of illegitimate children as low class. Even if adoptees have been given facts of superior heritage, the subtle disparagement which pervades their daily lives deflates all but the strongest and most secure individuals.

The fantasies start in early childhood and reach a peak in adolescence. For example, a five-year-old talked with conviction about a neighboring house where she was sure she was born and lived as a baby. A seven-year-old girl dreamed she was riding a motorcycle which went away with her into the sky. She felt she was a princess going to an unknown place. An ardent television watcher of eight dreamed she was the subject of a court battle between her birth mother and her adoptive parents. She was supposed to make a choice and woke up when she couldn't decide. A nine-year-old boy, helping to set the family table, carefully put the knives and spoons on the left side of the plate and the forks on the right. When questioned by his mother he explained, "This is the way my other mother set the table." He had been adopted at three weeks of age.

Fantasies in adolescence are less imaginative and more explicit. A boy who conceived of his birth parents as married enjoyed imagining the kind of house they lived in, thinking perhaps where he would fit into it. A sixteen-year-old girl born in war torn Asia dramatized herself as a product of rape between an American G.I. and a geisha girl. The claim brought her lots of attention from titillated peers.

One adolescent, struggling with his own sexuality, goodhumoredly pictured his mother having similar problems. "My mother had to be sexy like me or I wouldn't have gotten here." An adopted girl of fourteen came to her parents intensely shaken and in tears with a sudden realization, "I could pass my real mother on the street and I wouldn't even know her." Maybe she thought she had.

The answer to fantasy is fact. But who has the facts? Questions asked in early childhood and answered in generalities are asked again in adolescence. The questions are the same but have taken on new significance. More tangible answers are demanded. What can parents say now? They may never have been told the facts and probably did not anticipate the need for concrete answers. Neither did those social workers who told them nothing about their children's forebears.

The trouble starts with the notion that an adopted child will automatically take on the heritage of the adoptive parents and needs none of his own. Parents who conceive this to be the case may pass off what is told them about the baby as information meant only for them in order to decide whether to go ahead with the adoption. Or they may cut off the social worker's discourse to state, emphatically, "I don't care where the baby comes from. I just want a baby." They prefer to make a clean sweep of the past and incorporate the new family member as if of their own blood and heritage. Many parents manage to forget the facts they were told about their children's heritage and lose their notes during the sixteen years that pass between their children's adoption and their adolescence. Whether they have lost their notes deliberately or by accident, parents usually regret that they no longer have them.

Adoption workers are chiefly to blame for the paucity of facts which may be made available for questioning adolescents. They have been indoctrinated, as have parents, that adopted children being the same as biological children take their heritage from their adopters. Social workers, assumed to be sensitive to human problems, should have been the first to realize the needs of adopted adolescents for true facts about themselves. It remains a sober responsibility of the adoption workers to gather, record and make the facts available. It is not always easy to do so.

Often the social worker must cajole and wheedle information from the birth parents. The problem sometimes rests with the birth mother herself. She may be young, preoccupied with her pregnancy and too confused and inarticulate to want to talk about family history. Out of loyalty, fear or ignorance of his whereabouts, she may fail to identify the birth father or to reveal anything about him. Few birth mothers can visualize the years ahead, so caught up are they with the serious concerns of the moment. Anticipating future needs of their unborn infants is beyond the scope of their comprehension. Only if pointed out by a far-seeing social worker will they understand that their own heritage belongs also to their offspring; that as birth mothers of babies to be adopted, they must grant their children the ultimate benefaction of a known family heritage. Non-professionals in the business of adoption, even more than agency workers, fail to anticipate the importance of heritage to the adoptee.

Many adopters hesitate to ask questions at the time of placement out of fear that any demands will be met with rebuffs and that their questions will be held against them. They are terrified of displeasing the omnipotent social worker and losing the baby.

Parents share background information with their adolescent children in different ways and at different times. Unless their children ask, parents may postpone telling them what they know until the last moment as they go off to college or leave to get married.

One adoptive mother answering her daughter's questions put it this way, "I know a lot about you which I will tell you when you are older. You will be very happy to hear the nice things I have to say, but this is not the appropriate time." One parent felt that the histories of her children belonged privately to each one of them. She explained, "I will tell each of you, when you are old enough, all about yourselves and then if there is something you wish to share with each other, that will be up to you."

Another mother held the view that as long as her daughter did not seem to be upset and did not ask any questions there was no need to tell her anything, in spite of the fact that her daughter had, as she expressed it, "a beautiful background." She believed knowing would *not* contribute to her daughter's feeling of well-being and would merely confuse her. Maybe like another adopter, she was waiting for that unspecified time when "the impact will be greater and the significance understood."

Secure parents seem to be able to incorporate their children's birth heritage into daily life without self-consciousness. As a result the children grow up with a good feeling about both their adoptive and birth parents. One example will illustrate the ease with which one father talked about his son's birth parents. The father was struggling to put together a broken drill. His son had a natural aptitude which his father lacked. In audible sighs of exasperation the father turned to his son and said, "You are so clever, so much more mechanical than your old Dad. It must have come from the other side of the family, from your other parents."

Adoptees themselves can make it difficult for their parents to share information with them. As in adolescence they become preoccupied with themselves, they seek privacy in their thoughts. The barriers they erect may be impossible for their parents to breach. At this age they take little satisfaction in their adoptions. They often wish desperately they were birth children to their parents and push away the facts of their adoption. Although devoted and grateful to their parents, they may resent the extra obligation which adoption imposes on them. They no longer want outsiders to know.

Adolescents may resort to lying about their adoptions when curious strangers ask. By doing so they cut off further inquiry on a subject they want to forget. One boy of thirteen I talked to said, "My parents told me everything but it is like a story about someone else, not me. If I hadn't been told, I wouldn't have this feeling I was born to someone else. I wished they had never told me. I wish it wasn't true."

In response to their children's new sensitivity, the formerly proud and boasting parents of young adoptees are obliged to become reserved and evasive parents of adolescents. For example, one mother took great joy in her adopted daughter's resemblance to her and always shared the extraordinary happenstance with anyone who noted it. But one day when she explained, "Yes she does look like me and isn't it remarkable since she is adopted," her twelve-year-old daughter, who had never minded before, became angry and incensed, "Why did you have to tell her I was adopted?" she protested. Her mother never did it again.

For adoptees who do not resemble their parents, the dissimilarity which formerly troubled them little becomes a sign post which tells the world they are adopted. They cannot escape the comment they come to hate, "How come you don't look like your folks?" Only when they leave home can they live in their own worlds, free from busybody strangers and reminders of their adoption.

The escape is never complete, however, for every adopted person must face the continual discomfort of being questioned by his physician about his family's medical history. If the adoptee lies and embraces the acquired medical history of his adopted family, he will save himself from further questioning but will lead the doctor astray. If he tells the truth, that he does not know his genetic history because he is adopted, he reaffirms that he is different from others.

In adolescence, adoptees reflect more deeply upon the adoption process. They recognize the element of chance that placed them in one family instead of another. It is unsettling especially for adoptees who feel they do not fit in with or measure up to their parents and siblings. The pain of not belonging can be acute for the introspective adoptee conscious that his membership in the family was made by human and not biological choice. One eighteen-year-old protested to his mother after my visit, "I wish she hadn't come. I don't like to think I'm adopted. Why do we have to talk about it anyway."

When adolescents begin to date they may keep their adoptions secret for fear of being confronted by ignorant and biased contemporaries they wish to please. If their affairs become more serious they may be confronted by the potential parents-in-law who will question the unknown heritage.

In the families of adolescent adoptees the mothers, rather than the fathers, bear the brunt of their children's self-assertive rebellion. But the adoptive mothers are not alone as the objects of their children's disdain, for birth mothers are equally unjustly abused.

Adoptive parents will be relieved to know that all adolescents do not have the temperament of one fourteen-year-old girl I talked to. This adoptee was fascinating and wildly difficult. She flaunted her disdain for her elders with rough manners and bold words. She was an embarrassing visitor to the neighbors and a crazy clown to her schoolmates. When I saw her, she wore wild-colored boys' shirts under torn and patched bib overalls, which were enormous for her wiry frame. Her dark hair flopped in disarray, but the embryonic signs of female vanity were beginning to emerge. Her long fingernails were painted green and her dirty bare feet displayed toenails painstakingly etched in black.

Her well-articulated abuse veered back and forth between her two mothers, weaving a pattern of vilification which was laughable in its excessiveness.

She told me about a dream she had had that scared her. "It was bad," she said, "This dark-haired witch woman came down the stairs into my room when I was sleeping. She went all over picking up things and pushing them around like she was trying to find something. I didn't know who it was. At first I thought it was my mother who's always picking up my room and now I'm not sure. It could have been my other mother."

Following up on the suggestion the dream had sparked she declared her birth mother as probably a "dumb woman, some sort of hag."

To her mother she had said: "If you were my real mother you wouldn't treat me this way. You didn't want me. You resent me because I'm not your own daughter. Why don't you find an orphanage that will take me and then send me there."

One day, trying to provoke her mother, this fourteen-year-old commented, "I think you should ask my real mother to my wedding." To her surprise her mother replied, "I think that would be very nice. I would like to meet her and I think she would like to come." Defeated in her attempt to stir up her adoptive mother, she shifted back to her birth mother. "She'd never want to come. You know what she'd say?" and in a sarcastic tone she went on, "She'd say 'Thanks a lot'."

I asked her how she felt about my having placed her in her home. "Sure I'm just as glad you put me here. I'd hate to be in some snob family like next door. You know my mother can be pretty cool sometimes."

The qualities of determination and dissent in this fourteen-year-old are, I am sure, sweeping her toward her destiny as a reformer. Difficult, interesting and amusing, I feel she'll be heard from. Her mother is convinced she should be the first president of "child liberation."

The answer to the demanding and accusing adopted adolescent may be best summed up by an exasperated mother who told her son, "You will just have to put up with your family. You'll have to live with our disapproval and realize it does not mean we don't love you. We are stuck with each other. We are just as stuck with you as you are with us."

Outbursts in adolescence are not constant. Weeks of peace go by without rebellious episodes. And there are adopted adolescents who seem to have come to terms with themselves and, in a mature way, are masters of their adoptive situation.

I talked with one eighteen-year-old girl about to set off for college from a home where open discussion was combined with loving concern. She was a straight-forward, confident, intelligent and well-organized leader of her peer group. She had never minded being different. She explained to me, "First I was fat, then I was crazy, and now with my best friend I sometimes act like a monkey and a retard." She regarded adoption factually. She explained, "My parents wanted a child. Someone else had me. The story of my life is like a movie. It's no big thing." She remembered that when she felt misunderstood she would imagine her biological parents understanding her better than her adopters. But she never felt resentful at being given up by her birth parents, and was fascinated rather than self-conscious about her adoption. She joked about it, kidding her father about the "other woman" (her alleged birth mother). She sometimes imagined that she might be the daughter of some prominent Washington figure. She thought it would be fun to embarrass a pretentious politician by walking in on him and announcing her relationship as his illegitimate child. When an unwitting schoolmate swore at her and yelled "You bastard," she calmly retorted "How did you know?"

She told me about giving a speech in school on "Adoption not Abortion" and said, "The teacher got all psychological, and talked about how heart-rendering it must have been for my birth mother. I was disgusted with all that sentimentality. If I ever meet my biological mother, I hope she won't be sentimental like that."

"Adoption," she said, "is like a birthmark. It should be treated openly not hidden. It's easy to adjust to being different. It's like being Chinese or black, not that important."

She would like to meet her biological parents, especially her mother who, she had been told, was interested in political science. "I'd be curious to know whether she carried through on her education, whether she went into politics, but I wouldn't want to hurt her if she didn't want to see me. I'm curious, but I'm not looking for a mother. I've got one."

There are irreconcilable conflicts for adoptive parents, faced with questions from their adolescent children for which there are no satisfactory answers. How does a parent separate the birth mother as a whole person, with whom an adoptee may identify, from the birth mother as a sexual aberrant? How does a parent retain a positive view of her child's birth mother while censuring her out-of-wedlock pregnancy? How does a parent explain her thankfulness for the birth mother's transgression at the same time that she warns her child against repeating the pattern of pregnancy out-of-wedlock? How can parents lucky enough to have adopted children in 1965 be crusaders for abortions in 1975?

Attempts to handle the sexual education of their children may be difficult for adopters, not only because of their childrens' illegitimate beginnings but because of their own unfulfillment as birth parents.

Adopted adolescents are raised like others according to the double standard. Boys are allowed to choose their friends and to wander unsupervised, while girls are watched and their friendships censored. The difference is not entirely cultural. The cause is founded on the earthy fact that girls get pregnant and boys do not. Sex and pregnancy are realistically linked in the minds of adopters. The specter of birth mothers pregnant in their teens nettles the parents' consciousness, and they worry about recurrent patterns in their daughters. As their adolescent daughters turn inward, parents are left to wonder whether identity with birth mothers and a susceptibility to strong sexual drives will prove greater than the model they have tried to inculcate. Preoccupied with the possibility of their daughters' teenage pregnancies, fathers I have known seem needlessly strict and punitive in their discipline.

One forthright mother explained to her adolescent children, "Being responsible is the answer to your questions about sex.

Illegitimate pregnancy is a mistake of love. All mothers love their babies but they are hurt when they bear children out of wedlock. They are no more promiscuous or immoral than the fathers of the babies, but they are the ones who suffer." She explained to one son, "Sex is like fire. It can burn you or warm you. If you love a girl you will be willing to wait."

Another mother put it this way. "I have always tried to give my children a sense of the great worth of family life. The institution of the family is the ideal basis for human existence." She explained to her growing adolescent children, "Sex need not be related to pregnancy. It is a lovely way for two people who are in love to express their feelings for each other." She pointed out that thirteen and fourteen-year-olds were mature enough physically to produce children but they were too young to establish families. "Your friend Pamela seems very old for her age but she is only thirteen and doesn't know how to be a real mother any more than her boy friend could make a home and support her. They may think they want to keep their baby but they are not old enough yet."

This mother neither belittled the sexual expressions of birth parents nor the children's illegitimate beginnings. Instead she credited the birth parents with values like her own. "Your first parents felt just as Daddy and I do. We think that all children should grow up in families with mothers and fathers that can look after them when they are small and help them when they are older. Your other parents thought so too and that is why they arranged for you to be adopted."

11   REJECTION

ALL FIVE CHILDREN OF CAPTAIN and Mrs. Bartlett were adopted. Each one came to the Bartletts in a different way, one from an orphanage in Korea, one from a public welfare department in Texas, one from a state agency in Germany, one from a privately supported adoption agency in Washington, and the last through private sources.

The various ways the children were adopted, like the assorted houses the Bartletts bought and sold, were testimony to their way of life. Moving every two or three years was exciting and adventurous for them but a handicap in creating a family.

Adoption was a prolonged and anxious experience. Limited as they were by time, the Bartletts had to deal with dilatory social workers loath to consider families on the move. But their eagerness, persistence, and luck brought them five lovely children as different from each other as the processes of adoption had been.

The parents's knowledge of the children's backgrounds varied with the source of their adoptions. In one case, they had received a complete description of the birth mother and father, the grandparents, the medical history, and the reason that the baby was placed in adoption. In the case of another child, they knew only that his mother was German and his father American.

To Capt. and Mrs. Bartlett the backgrounds of their children had been immaterial, but as time passed and the children wanted answers to their questions, the parents regretted the casual way in which they had dismissed and forgotten the information offered them at the time of the adoptions.

Mrs. Bartlett sought to satisfy her children's inquiries with the various shreds of information she could remember, but when they asked "Why did my mother give me up", she hesitated because she knew that this question struck at the heart of adoption. Whether for reasons of poverty, illegitimacy or youth, the birth mothers in Mrs.

Bartlett's mind, had rejected their offspring. She could neither understand nor explain it.

Impossible for her to comprehend how any mother could give up a baby, she found herself unable to justify the deed with compassion. In the cases of only two of her children was she able to recall the particular circumstances leading to their adoptions. Knowing nothing of the reasons for the surrender of her other three, she was troubled by giving the facts to two children only. She felt it important to preserve equality between the children even with their dissimilar histories, so she turned the question back to her children.

"I don't know why your mothers didn't keep you, but maybe each of you can think of some good reasons.

Mrs. Bartlett was taken aback by the off hand way in which the children pondered what was to her a solemn matter. From each child a spontaneous explanation came forth.

"I bet they were killed in an auto accident," said the ten-year-old autobuff.

"Mine had too many babies already," announced the eight-year old, jealous of her younger brother.

"That's silly. My mother and father just weren't married," retorted the practical thirteen-year-old.

"I don't think they had enough to eat," said the hungry six-year-old.

"Well I know for sure my mother thought I was too ugly to keep," the self-deprecating fifteen-year-old declared.

The rejection of her children by their birth mother had seemed to Mrs. Bartlett a tough and everlasting injury from which her adopted children would forever suffer. She had vowed to cushion them as much as she could from the hurtful consequences. As her children described their trials by rejection, Mrs. Bartlett's solicitude dissolved into amused appreciation as she listened to each of them mirror their own self-absorbed individuality. They seemed less concerned by the fact of rejection than she was by the concept of it.

— — — — — — — — — —

Rejection is a strong and devastating word, a term employed frequently and loosely by psychologists and social workers. As used by them, rejection implies total repudiation, no whites or grays but absolute devaluation of one person by another. In adoption, the word rejection carries additional inquity. It is an unnatural act, the forsaking of a child by its mother, severing the closest relationship in the human experience. No wonder parents are appalled by the thought of their children's rejection and find the fact hardest to justify and explain.

"Why did my mother give me away?" "Why didn't the other lady keep me?" "Didn't my first mother want me?" These are hard questions for parents to answer. Parents are particularly anxious that their children not be hurt by the knowledge that their birth mothers abandoned them. Those who are unsympathetic with the birth mother are unable to interpret the situation for their children. For the experience of adopters is at variance with that of the unmarried mother. Adoptive parents who are securely married, who have gone through so much to have their desperately wanted children, cannot put themselves in the place of the very young women who without problems of sterility find themselves pregnant and unmarried. Adopters cannot fathom how a mother, no matter what the circumstances, could give up her baby.

Questions about the reasons birth mothers gave them away are usually asked by children seven or eight years of age. Some children inquire at a later age, and others never ask at all. A seven-year-old inquiring about his birth mother is seldom mature enough to sense the personal implications of rejection and abandonment. If he is a member of a loving adoptive family his questions probably spring from curiosity only. But the parents, with mature sensitivity, are apt to read into their children's questions implications to which they are emotionally attuned but which their children cannot perceive.

Even those parents who actually have specific information seem to prefer giving their children generalized answers, such as, "She couldn't find a way to keep you." For a seven-year-old, a simple answer may be sufficient, but later on only the specific circumstances leading to the surrender will satisfy the inquiring grown adoptee. Unfortunately few parents have the facts to give, and to some, having no facts means there is no need of discussion. They are relieved of responsibility because the agency failed to share information with them, or if their children came to them through the grey or black market, because information was undoubtedly non-existent. Passively taking only the information they were given, most parents failed to provide for the future needs of their children by not demanding more. One frequently hears a mother in answer to her child's inquiry about why he was given up say, "I really don't know. The agency never told me." The agencies are, of course, the chief culprits in not sharing all they know of the surrendering of the children by the birth parents.

A few parents, even if they are aware of the circumstances leading to the relinquishment of their children, are convinced that it is better for the children if the period before adoption is blotted out once and for all. They draw a curtain on any discussion about birth parents. Some of these mothers are afraid of allowing the birth mothers a place in the children's minds which rivals their own.. A threatened mother might hastily cut off discussion in a tone so sharp that a child will withdraw and ask nothing further. The effect on an adopted child unsympathetically put down by overreacting parents is destructive of his self image. He is left with the impression that there must have been something wrong with him to have caused his birth parents not to want to keep him. The adoptee's sense of rejection is greatly reinforced by the negative reaction of the parents.

Avoiding the unpleasant issue of rejection, some parents falsely picture the birth parents as dead. They sincerely feel that they are ridding their children of speculation and futile dreams about first parents who are alive and dwelling somewhere out in the world. Actually they may have introduced a more onerous vision for their children to dwell upon: the responsibility for their parents' deaths. A mother's death during childbirth is a dramatic and actual occurrence, in real life as well as on television, and an adopted child can easily imagine it. Furthermore, the fear for adopted children of a repeated pattern of losing parents may focus not on the possibility of a second rejection, which is a common obsession with growing adoptees, but on the specter of their adoptive parents' decease.

An adopted child's basic uncertainty may be impossible to totally dislodge, since our culture generally accepts the tenet that rejection goes hand in hand with adoption. This is the basis on which some mothers conclude that only by the unavoidable deaths of the birth parents, rather than by the deliberate surrender of their children, can the thoughts of rejection be erased from the children's minds.

It seems to be generally accepted by an ignorant public that the unmarried mother who relinquishes her child for adoption is fit for condemnation. She is abandoning and rejecting her own flesh and blood and casting off her maternal responsibilities. The child, unfortunately, must bear the rejection by his birth mother which is assumed to be the case, but the facts do not support the assumption of an unmarried mother's indifference to the child she surrenders for adoption.

I have witnessed hundreds of relinquishments of parental rights by married and unmarried mothers, and I can recall not more than a handful who did not suffer pangs of sorrow and remorse. In over nine hundred cases, only one child was actually abandoned, and then merely by the mother's failure to sign the papers of surrender after her child was safely in the agency foster home.

In the years of my experience, the principle reason for the surrender of children for adoption was not economic but social. Most unmarried mothers knew that adoption was a better alternative for their children and for themselves than keeping the children. In a society where their illegitimacy would be constantly thrown up to them, the innocent children, who were kept by their mothers would carry the heaviest scars. Adoptees who believe they were rejected by their birth mothers because they were not loved are quite mistaken.

Today, with our changing social climate, adoptees may be unable to comprehend that social pressure alone could have led to their being surrendered for adoption. Other more concrete reasons such as immaturity, pursuit of education and financial hardship may be more readily understood.

Today, when illegitimacy does not mark a child as it once did, a child born out of wedlock may be kept by a responsible mother with little damage. Yet adoption still shields the child more completely from his illegitimate status by providing the security of a whole family. The millions of children in the country who are fatherless through divorce, desertion and death are not fatherless in the same way as illegitimate children. Those born out of wedlock seldom have an acknowledged father. Although birth certificates are no longer stamped with a large "illegitimate" across the face, there is usually a blank space where the father's name should be. The child without a legally recorded father cannot have the same sure social status as other fatherless children. Some mothers in my study thought the illegitimacy of their children was more destructive of their self-worth than the thought of rejection by their birth mothers.

To combat the sense of rejection, I believe that adoptive parents must have an appreciative understanding of the birth parents. With this conviction in mind, I tried to give the adopters a true and vivid picture of the birth parents as human beings, with their personal struggles as well as their triumphs. I tried to make them real people to the adopters, always emphasizing their positive characteristics. The impression of the birth parents I conveyed may have been the greatest single benefit I granted the children as they moved on into their adoptive homes. For to downgrade birth parents is destructive to the child's image of himself, and in the long run it destroys his relationships with his parents. A mother who presumes that the birth mother deliberately rejected her child is disowning the heritage that belongs to her child; which, in fact, is her child.

Wise mothers, aware of the label, "rejected", their children carry, emphasize the birth mothers' love for them. One mother explained, "Your first mother loved you. She wanted you to have a home with a mother and father. Maybe she could not give you a real home. What she decided for you made us the lucky ones." To an angry outburst from her son, "My mother didn't want me", another mother explained "Your first mother was unable to care for you at the time you were born, and, although she tried, she could find no way to keep you. People's lives can be so difficult and confusing that it seems there is no way to do what one would like most to do."

A doubting ten-year-old refused to accept his mother's sympathetic explanation of his relinquishment by his birth parents. He was unmoved by her description of their youth and need for further schooling. He asked, "Were they married?" "No," replied his mother. "You mean I was illegal. They broke the law. Then I don't want to know them." His mother then explained how they had paid the price for breaking the rules. "They made a decision to protect you and the family institution. It must have been hard for them to give you up." At this her son who had known only love and approval changed his orientation. "Yes, that must have been awful, especially since it was me."

Children want to believe that their birth mothers are good rather than malevolent. They provoke comment in order to be reassured by their parents. Inquiring of his birth mother, an adoptee declared, "She couldn't have been a very nice lady if she didn't keep me." His mother replied, "She was a generous person, thinking only of what was best for you. She denied herself so that you could be brought up in a family." The idea of love and sacrifice by the first mother is more gratifying for the adoptee than the off-hand reply the mother might have given, such as, "I don't know what kind of lady she was, but I'm glad she didn't keep you anyway." Such statements, which show no feeling for the birth mother, merely confirm to the adopted child the casual indifference he believes his birth mother felt toward him, reinforcing his unworthiness as an unwanted and rejected child. In silent reflection, he may think himself just like her. Some adopted children go so far as to identify with and act out the delinquent behavior they believe typified their birth parents.

Demands for reassurance do not necessarily cease when the adoptee is old enough to know all the facts about his birth parents and their surrender of him. Leading questions, such as, "Why did you pick me?" "But you're my real mother?" "Why should I care about that other lady, she didn't care for me?", ask that parents repeat the events the adoptee already knows so well. He needs to counteract his momentary loss of faith in himself as a loved person. One mother was entirely comfortable and comforting in relating to her teenage daughter, "Your first mother loved you so much she could hardly bear to give you up. I understand she went back again and again to the foster home where you were to see you just one more time."

Typically, teenage girls believe their mothers do not understand them. Adopted teenage girls can have an even more exaggerated notion of their mother's lack of insight, for their mothers were not adopted and couldn't know how it feels. The closeness between mother and daughter of earlier years disappears as the adopted girl retreats into her world of fantasy, emerging only to explode with abusive harangues. A very dramatic instance of a renewal of the close relationship between a mother and her adopted daughter was told me by one mother.

The mother had taken her daughter to a family funeral, and after the service they had lingered in the graveyard. Together mother and daughter looked silently down upon the grave of the child's grandmother. She had died a young woman years before, leaving her small child (now the grown adopter) motherless. Momentarily overcome, the usually staunch adoptive mother wept openly for the mother she could not remember. The daughter was stunned by her mother's grief. Noticing that her daughter was suddenly very quiet, the mother, in a flash of insight, was struck by the similarity of their circumstances. Both had lost their birth mothers at an early age and had been raised by substitute mothers. She did not bury her thoughts in silence, but instinctively shared her revelations with her daughter. They sorrowed together in their first deeply mutual affinity. The daughter's emotional encasement was relieved and her mindless rebellion against her mother ceased.

Sympathizing with the birth mother and understanding the problems and decisions she had to face is difficult for adopters whose lives are limited in variety of human experiences. Parents who attempt to interpret the feelings of the birth mothers to their adopted children are lost in their ignorance. Many cannot picture the birth mother as a person with whom they would ever have been acquainted. One adoptive mother helped her children understand their own place in the adoption scene, by opening her home to unwed expectant mothers. The children were able to see at first hand the circumstances of life from which the institution of adoption springs.

One of the young daughters in the family was awed by an attractive unwed mother who had just brought her baby home from the hospital. She was impressed by the strong love of the mother for her infant, but also with the mother's confusion and emotional turmoil about whether to keep the baby. As the weeks went on, she came to see the baby as the victim of a capricious and inattentive parent, who was too immature to carry the responsibility of motherhood. It was she, the adopted daughter, who prevailed upon the birth mother to seek adoption for the baby.

The fact that we seek reasons to explain why a mother relinquishes her child for adoption implies that rational considerations are utilized in the decision. But the pros and cons of the immediate situation cannot be easily weighed, and their application to the future life situations of both mother and child is a gamble. Harrowing as the decision is for the new mother, her immediate predicament and her instinctive desire to do right by the baby determine her move to surrender her child.

Often helping a mother to unravel her other problems releases her to look to the life of her child with greater clarity. An example in a mother's own words demonstrates how guidance led to a decision which she explained in a letter for her child:

"During my first three days in the hospital I couldn't eat or sleep and was on the verge of exhaustion, until a very wonderful social worker, God bless her, advised me to see a priest, and I talked to him about you. I don't remember how long we talked, but after our conversation ended I had gained peace of mind and soul. I shall never forget the priest's words, 'You have had a boy. Remember that only you and God could have given him life. God had a reason for things to go this way. The boy will be baptized a Catholic and will be adopted into a good Catholic home by parents who have waited and prayed for a son, parents that will love and cherish him until eternity. You have not committed a sin. You have borne God's child.' " Comforted by the priest she was able to relinquish her child without guilt. She wrote further:

"That, my child, is the reason I gave you up for adoption. I shall have a prayer in my heart forever for you and your parents. They have done more for you than I could ever do. They both prayed to God so long for you and finally through me, he sent them to you. Cherish them always. Please try to understand what I have written, and if you feel malice towards me, try to remember that I shall always love you and that wherever you go, my prayers shall go with you. I pray that I shall some day see you in heaven, but until we meet, Go with God."

Another unmarried mother wrote a letter to her son attempting to explain her reasoned decision, trusting that when he was grown the agency would give the letter to him. "While I held you in my arms you looked directly at me and when I sang a little lullaby to you, I'm sure I saw you smile. I loved you, my son, loved you with a fierce but tender maternal animal passion that had nothing in common with the steady, constructive love that you have received from your parents. Many months prior to your birth I had made arrangements were a fine agency for your adoption. I had known from the time I knew I was pregnant that I could not morally keep you as my own, and therefore I had not made the dreams and plans for you that the usual mother makes for her children. Thus I was spared the heartbreak of parting with you that so many mothers have suffered when their children were taken from them because of wars, or too little money or, worst of all, death.

"Do you know the Old Testament story of the two women who appeared before King Solomon, each claiming the same baby as her son? Solomon said: 'Bring me a sword and divide the living in two, and give half to one and half to the other.' The first woman pled with the King not to slay the boy, but to give him to the second woman. The second woman said "No, divide the boy." Then Solomon knew the first woman was the real mother, and gave the boy to her. I would not have you divided, my son. Your birthright was to have two parents to love you and care for you and lead you in the paths of honorable manhood."

"You gave me life by giving me motherhood, and I gave it back to you by giving you parents, confident that with them you will have gained all the happiness and known all the love that you could not have received alone from your natural mother."

12 GENETIC HERITAGE

SARAH WAS ADOPTED WHEN SHE WAS four months old. Her adoption had been delayed by a search for parents who would accept her, a "hard-to-place" baby. The medical tests done before her adoption showed normal development, but her birth history of long delayed breathing could have caused brain damage. As she grew, Sarah might become spastic. She could be retarded. All considerations of finding adopters with social background similar to hers became secondary as we searched for the rare couple with qualities of faith and compassion who would give her a home.

We found them: an unsophisticated family-oriented young couple, who shared basic good sense, warmth and humor. Their ultimate goal in life was to have a family, to provide for their children, to grow with them, and to be available to them in good times and bad. They wished their children to become upstanding adults, and later on to have children of their own.

Both adopters were high school graduates. The father, a mechanic, was a responsible, conscientious worker, who, with two jobs, had saved enough to purchase the property on which he built the family home. The mother—laundress, cook, seamstress, nurse, and counselor—was a cheerful homemaker.

Eventually they adopted three children. Sarah was the first. She has grown up free of the dire medical complications we had anticipated. Ten years had elapsed between her placement and my next visit. Her mother told me about her extraordinary daughter.

Sarah was an active girl scout, secretary of her class, an A student, an inveterate reader, a poet. Her special heroine was Helen Keller, whose life story she had read in every biography the town library possessed. She had blindfolded her eyes for several hours to understand better how it would feel to be blind. She was learning Braille and sign language. She observed people with a sensitive spirit.

One day she asked her mother, "Why don't they have library shelves lower so people in wheelchairs can reach the books?" Her mother commented, "People could always ask the librarian to reach the books for them." "But that would hurt their dignity," her daughter replied.

Sarah's compassion for the handicapped and her sensitivity to those less fortunate than herself could have come directly from the environment of her adoptive home. But her intellectual curiosity and her personal ambitions were far different from those of her parents. Although they feared she might grow away from them as her education progressed, her parents encouraged Sarah and were proud of her. Her mother reflected thoughtfully, "Sarah's already smarter than I am. We never could have had such a child born to us."

– – – – – – – – – –

Psychologists studying the effects of environment on children's development have placed the formative period nearer and nearer the children's birth dates and are most recently following infants into their mother's wombs.

Years ago the expression, "Give me a child before he is seven," taught us that by seven years of age a child's basic character would be formed. Subsequently the prime time for shaping personality has been progressively reduced to three months. Now studies by psychologists are moving even further back to learn the effects on child development of the pre-natal period. The environmental psychologists are hesitant to go all the way, however, and give principle credit to genetic determination at the moment of conception. But the distinctive personalities of new-born infants have been observed by nurses and foster mothers for years. To what degree these early characteristics are modified by the environment is interesting to speculate about.

Adopted children, born of parents who give them their heritage and raised by parents who provide their environment, should furnish a testing ground for the relative influences of heredity and environment on human personality. It is a fascinating subject of an utterly complex nature. In curiosity, I tackled a study of two to three-year-old toddlers by questionnaires which I sent to their adoptive parents. The forty children had been observed by a foster mother during their time with her before adoption, which occurred when they were from four to six weeks of age. I found that infants who had shown extremes of temperament in the foster home, such as hyperactivity, unusual passivity or high temper, still retained these characteristics at age three. All children considered "serious" by their parents were found to be sober infants at four weeks. Aggressive and non-aggressive behavior in the children appeared unrelated to their infant activity or to their sex. Most interesting were the findings of the children with high vocabularies. They were not the infants who were especially alert and responsive in the foster home but rather the quiet, good-natured, contented babies.

Most adoption workers take little note of the hereditary qualities of children to be adopted. The psychiatrically biased social worker has such faith in the dominance of environment that she shuns heritage as a factor in choosing families for infants she places in adoption. Furthermore as she loses touch with the adoptive family soon after placement, she has no way of observing the adoptee as he grows and develops. She sincerely believes that adoptive children will be, without question, a reflection of their new parents.

Generally, adoptive parents also avoid viewing their children as products of their natural heritage. In making the children their own through adoption, they guardedly ignore the birth families as sources of the personalities and talents their children possess.

Skeptical of the orthodoxy of environmentalists, I tried to place children with adoptive families that closely resembled the families from which they were born. It seemed obvious that if the hereditary factors proved a strong element in the children, there would be fewer problems for them with parents of similar backgrounds. In searching for the potential of the babies to be adopted, I often found that their grandparents gave a clearer picture of the possibilities than the young birth parents whose immaturity concealed their innate qualities. If the child's background could not be known or if my assumption of the importance of heritage proved false, then at least the environmental influences of a good home would still provide the security for any child placed there.

The evidence of genetic determination is most clearly seen in familiar diseases such as muscular dystrophy, Huntington's disease and hemophilia. One may be predisposed by biological relationship to schizophrenia, diabetes or pernicious anemia. Or one may be racially marked with Tay-Sacks disease or sickle-cell anemia. Where does one draw the line between what is innate and what is acquired?

In returning to observe adoptees after years in their adoptive homes, I have seen that they are still largely the offspring of their biological parents, not only in outward appearance but in their interests and character. I don't have answers, only observations. They show me that an adoptive environment may modify development but does not change the essential nature with which the adoptee is born.

I have noted that adopted children frequently have unusual talents which nobody in the adoptive family is familiar with or possesses. I have noted that mixed-race babies appear more lively and brighter than either of their birth parents. Parents often protest that they cannot imagine where their children's gifts come from.

In seeing adoptees again after twenty years, I have been able in many cases to associate them with the birth parents I remember. My early cases, which these adoptions represent, stand out most vividly in my memory and make the linkage possible. I saw striking evidence of the dominance of inherited traits in many instances.

Lucy was adopted by a city couple whose activities centered on cultural interests, the theatre, ballet and politics. Intellectually liberal, they were conservative in their style of living. But not Lucy. She was wedded to the outdoors, to the fields and woods, to insects and animals and to all growing things. By birth she came from a line of naturalists. Her grandfather was a veterinarian.

Jim was a confused adolescent, struggling to find himself in an environment where private schools, valuable contacts, and innumerable opportunities were his for the asking. Nothing held his attention for long until the day he went sailing for the first time. He was intrigued and absorbed in the boat, sails, ropes, and manoeuvres in the wind. He was descended from five generations of sailors and boat builders.

Victoria had always shown great facility with language. In grammar school her themes were read aloud in class. In high school her stories were published in the school paper. A highly motivated English student in college, she earned her spending money writing for a local newspaper. Her parents looked upon their paragon with uncomprehending pride. Victoria's birth mother had appeared a bewildered teenager, but her maternal grandfather was a veteran newspaper correspondent.

Irene was explosive. In anger, she streaked to her room and slammed the door. In sorrow, she wept without control. She was perceptive and aware, verbalizing rather than keeping her feelings to herself. Observing her fellow humans, she responded to their behavior with insight and emotion. Her family called her "Sarah

Bernhardt." Her parents were not at all surprised to learn that Irene's mother was a student of the theatre and her father a drama teacher.

George was an obstreperous roughneck, admired by his peers for his defiance of authority. He kept his sensitive, gentle qualities well hidden beneath his adolescent rebelliousness. At fifteen he asked to be given music lessons. By seventeen he was hooked on the piano. His progress was phenomenal and his teacher was awed by his talent. In his adoptive family no one was musically sophisticated but in his birth family his maternal grandmother had been a concert pianist.

The examples of the forces of heredity are uncanny and numberless: the beautifully-coordinated athlete now training for the Olympics, whose birth father was a medal winner there the year before she was born; the boy leader in the band whose father played in the symphony orchestra; the child with the mechanically-skilled head and hands whose father was an inventor; the able young mathematician whose mother I found reading a treatise on symbolic logic the day after he was born.

One bright and serious young adoptee assessed his environment and his heredity thus: "My father has only average intelligence but he is psychologically strong. As for my natural parents, I think I am like them, factual and not imaginative. My interest in them is one of genetics only."

Adoptive parents may be told of particular abilities of the birth families and thus anticipate their children's talents. Others are baffled by their children's personalities which they do not understand yet often feel responsible for. Sometimes puzzled adoptive parents return to the agency to become reacquainted with birth parents through the information in closed records so that they may understand their child better. One case stands out in my mind.

Tom, at eight, was an anxious child. He cried when he was left alone. He was afraid of the dark. He feared the police. He was terrified of fire and thunderstorms. Excitable and tense, he demanded attention, was impatient with delay and unstrung when denied. His volatile personality was utterly foreign to his steady, genial parents. In the easy world of their families, there had never been a member so impetuous and unpredictable. They looked for the problem within themselves, surmising that they were in some way handling their son badly. They sought the advice of a family counselor. Reassuring as the counselor was, the greatest consolation came from a review of their son's heritage. The file revealed that both Tom's birth parents were high strung individuals. The inevitable breakup of these two agitated people had released Tom for other parents to raise, but did not free him from the stamp of his lineage.

Young adoptive couples relate their children's interests and talents to themselves, just as young adoptees also identify with their acquired surroundings. Biological heritage is obscured in family affection and pride, at least temporarily. But as their children grow older, most parents come to recognize how much their children's individuality is born in them. To some their children are like strangers in the family setting. Some parents are intimidated by their children's obvious capabilities. Others are disappointed by their failure to meet parental expectations. The luckiest children are those whose parents allow them room to grow in their own innate ways.

Grown adopted children know full well that their adoptive heritage is not their own. They come to feel like outsiders in families where ancestor worship and class snobbery pervade. Those who are very unlike their adopters may have a particularly strong sense of not belonging. There is only one course for parents to take: open discussion of true heritage and acceptance of differences between their children and themselves.

The one item of heritage which all adopters seem to know and find themselves comfortable in sharing is their children's nationality and racial origins. As their children grow and reveal themselves, parents fall into the habit of relating their children's personalities to their national origins rather than to their birth families. They may credit their child's compulsiveness to his German heritage, his moodiness to the Scandinavian ancestry, or his volatile disposition to the Italian in him.

Some adopted children enjoy the game of seeing themselves as nationality types. Siblings refer to each other in jest as "Kraut" "wop" and "Italian lover." A young adoptee combined her birth and adoptive heritage into one and called herself "Germish" for German and Irish. There is also of course the usual adoptee's fantasy of being an Indian or Arabian prince or princess.

Some parents ignore even national heritage and explain their children's personalities through astrology: Leo the leader, Taurus the stubborn, and Cancer the domestic. One of the most common requests from parents after the records of their children have been filed away is to be told the exact hour and minute of their children's births. I soon learned that the moment of parturition was a most important item to obtain from the hospital and to share with star-gazing parents.

One of the pleasures of parenthood is watching the growth of babies taking their first unsteady steps to becoming well-coordinated teenagers, of babbling infants maturing into articulate adults. The development of children whose personalities gradually unfold and are revealed brings both pain and pride to parents. For adoptive parents, the mysteries are greater and the discoveries more surprising because adopters come into parenthood with children whose heritages are elusive. Like diggers for treasure in the desert, the special joys of discovery are theirs. If they can make their way from measles to marriage, adopters will know that they have been true participants in the human experience of parenthood.

13   UNUSUAL ADOPTIONS BECOME USUAL

BY THE TIME DAVID WAS THREE years old, he was emotionally handicapped. His mother, deserted by her husband when David was a baby, was the sole supporter of his older sister and himself. She had been dissuaded from considering adoption for David by friends who offered help but forgot their promises after the novelty and drama of the situation wore off. Other family members, already overburdened with their own problems, left her to solve hers. David's mother had two alternatives, to stay home with both children, inadequately supported by public welfare, or to take a job for which she was well-qualified and place David in a foster home. She was able to manage with her daughter, who was old enough to attend nursery school, but she was unsuccessful in planning for David's care at home.

His mother took the job and placed David, 15 months old, in a foster home of a county welfare department for what she thought would be a temporary arrangement. At first David's mother and sister visited regularly, but when it was necessary to transfer him to another foster home, the distance to the new home was too great for all but occasional trips. In the first months when they came, David would cling to them and cry when they left, but later he neither laughed nor cried when they came or went. Transferred to still another foster home, he became a withdrawn, apprehensive, and obedient boy. Internalizing his hurt, and his anger, he struck out through vomiting, throwing up his meals without any apparent cause. Irritating as it was to clean up after David, his foster mother could hardly punish such a quiet, non-aggressive little boy for a stomach upset. Hospitalized for a week, he was diagnosed as having allergies to certain foods and discharged to return to the foster home. He was beginning to feel at home there and the foster parents were becoming very fond of David. The vomiting had abated somewhat, but grew worse when his mother came. She was advised to spread out her visits, not to cause more trouble for David and his foster parents.

By the time David was three, the tie with his mother and sister was tenuous. His mother was torn between her guilt at sending him away and her bitterness that he no longer cared for her.

The crisis came when she learned that David's foster parents were moving to California. They would delay their departure until a plan was made for David, but they could no longer keep him. David's mother saw no end to disruptions for him, in being moved from one place to another. The physical separation of mother and son had already brought about an emotional separation between them. She saw no answer but adoption. She blamed herself for not having foreseen the damage she had done David in trying to keep him.

It took three months to locate David's father and to gain his consent to the adoption. Prospective parents had been found who waited eagerly to meet David. After the papers of surrender had been signed and filed in court, David was brought to the office to see his prospective parents. Adoption, still unsettled, was not mentioned to David by anyone.

David came with his social worker for the meeting with the adopters. He was suspicious of the group of eager adults surrounding him. Tense and observing, he uttered only monosyllables. The prospective parents tried to ease his discomfort to no avail. David left after an hour's visit, still mute and sober, but tightly clutching a talking bear the adopters had given him. The meeting appeared to be a disaster. We looked to the adopting parents for their reaction. They found David's behavior sensitive and understandable. They wanted him to be their son.

But what about David? Would these parents be his choice? David was taken home still holding his talking bear. His foster mother greeted him with the question, "David, where did you get that beautiful bear?" "Oh," said David, "my Daddy gave it to me."

David was adopted. His reticence gave way to aggressiveness. He provoked his parents to test their love. He fought with the other children in the family. His insecurity took a long time to abate. But he never punished his adoptive parents. He never threw up his meals again.

————————

Twenty years ago, children considered hard-to-place included the mentally retarded, "older" children (over two years), racial minorities, and those with physical impairments, such as cleft palates, club feet, and heart defects. In order to encourage the adoption of handicapped children, attempts were made to correct the physical anomolies before the children were presented to prospective parents. Later it became customary to place babies with correctable defects while they were still infants, so that psychological deprivation would not be added to their physical problems. The parents preferred to take on the medical care of defective children themselves, and to have them as their own from infancy. The mentally retarded children were, and still are, the hardest to find homes for. Many of the severely affected are more appropriately taken into institutions.

The unadoptable child of yesterday is no longer hard to place. The paucity of healthy infants for adoption has made it possible for the older child, the handicapped child and the minority and mixed race children to be adopted into permanent homes. Only the children who need the protection of institutional care or for whom adoption will be no benefit are considered unadoptable today.

Black children in the fifties were generally adopted only by parents of the same race. The shortage of black adopters resulted in healthy black babies in the District of Columbia being unadoptable. Attempts to promote and ease adoption for black couples had been increasingly successful, but the numbers of black adopters is still inadequate to the need. Adoption in the United States is still primarily a custom of the white race.

In the adoption agency, one looks upon the parents who take the hard-to-place children with gratitude and sometimes awe. What constitutes a handicap is seen quite differently by individual adopters.

A couple with strong religious convictions might ignore the negative warnings of a geneticist and adopt a child with a poor prognosis, with faith that love and a miracle would cure him. Other couples would be quite comfortable with a defect that did not show, like a congenital heart condition, but were put off by the appearance of a defective limb. People who were themselves afflicted did not necessarily want to adopt children who were similarly handicapped; for example the blind and deaf. Athletic parents found they could not accept crippled children, with club feet or palsy, who would be unable to participate in their world of sports. Most black parents could not accept infants with kinky hair or those whose skin would become darker than their own. Looking behind the ears of newborn light skinned infants, the black parents could foresee the darker shade of color the babies would eventually have.

Not all physical handicaps are permanent of course. There are ingenious corrections devised every year to rid children of congenital defects, and many adopting parents are encouraged by the hope that medical developments will provide cures for their handicapped children.

I recall one infant with a severe heart condition who was adopted by a doctor and his wife years before any operation had been devised to close the hole in his heart. The specialist who examined the baby and the doctor who adopted him both counted on a corrective operation being perfected before the boy reached six. Otherwise his chance of ever growing up was slim. Five years later the operation was performed, and today the infant who came close to death during his first months is a healthy college sophomore.

There were occasionally couples who came to me asking specifically for children in greatest need. Two of the families adopted five children each, all with crippling mental and psychological problems, an undertaking beyond the scope of most people's comprehension. Both mothers belittled the additional daily labors the children's afflictions required, and somehow found their own reward.

The child I considered most difficult to place was a cretin. He was surrendered to us by his birth mother before the symptoms of cretinism were seen. His foster mother was the first to note subtle changes in his development which she brought to the attention of the agency pediatrician. As a result, thyroid therapy was begun early. From a rapid downward spiral into inert mindlessness, there was a gradual shift upward toward normal growth. The prognosis was guarded. Seven months went by. Progress was slow and no adopters came.

I was faced with the necessity of making permanent plans other than adoption for him. We had taken a relinquishment of parental rights for the baby's adoption only, but did not have the legal guardianship necessary for institutional or other care which only the mother could give. The mother had gone her way, satisfied that all was well and that she had made the right decision in having her son adopted. I had to find her. I found her listed in the local phone book as she had not left Washington and I hardened myself to the fact that on Tuesday evening I would call her at home.

On Tuesday morning the office phone rang, and a woman with a firm and cheerful voice inquired, "Do you have any children to adopt for whom there are no homes?" Without any expectation I told her about the cretin baby explaining the prognosis and treatment. "Oh" she said, identifying immediately with him, "I take thyroid too." Though her low metabolism was a far cry from his total absence of a thyroid gland, she and her husband were not appalled.

Eventually, after thorough agency investigation of the young couple and medical consultation between the doctor and the parents about the baby's chances for normalcy, the baby was taken home by his new parents. He was nine months old then, and sufficiently alert to note the change of environment. He cried for his familiar foster mother and, while he slept fitfully, his new mother held him in her arms and rocked him all through the first long night.

I never had to make the phone call to his birth mother. He is now a high school teenager. His congenital affliction neither took away his ability to bring joy to others nor obliterated his sense of humor.

Parents who adopt congenitally handicapped children have the unique advantage of raising their children without the guilt common to birth parents. The almost universal reaction of self blame suffered especially by the mothers of defective children is spared both the adopters and the children they raise. But no matter how reassuring adopters may be, most handicapped children are convinced that they were given up by their birth mothers because they were imperfect.

What motivates the families who ask to adopt problem children? Who adopts the hard-to-place infants when there are healthy ones available? What do the adopters derive from the extraordinary care and responsibility which they must give defective children? Parents who adopt unusual children are themselves unusual. They disdain appearances and conventional ways. They are not afraid, and resist the idea of playing safe. They have faith in themselves, even though on the surface they may appear artless and unsophisticated. They are endowed with a special grace which flows outwards to others less fortunate than they.

A religious mother will witness the confirmation of her faith as she witnesses each progressive episode in the growth of comprehension of her totally deaf son. The maternal woman will never have to relinquish the cloak of protective motherhood she carries with such ease and satisfaction, as her mongoloid daughter never grows up but remains forever a dependent child. The timid woman will grow in self-confidence and strength as she defends her crippled child against the abuse of his peers with indignation and fire. The challenged woman will be brought into a vast new world of expanding interests as she becomes involved in special schooling, mother's groups, campaigns, hospital benefits, and medical symposiums through the adoption of a spastic child.

The adopter's unquestioned interest in taking a hard-to-place child is essential to the favorable outcome of such adoptions. In private adoptions, the selection of parents is haphazard and the birth of a healthy pink and white baby is taken for granted. When an unmarried mother, planning adoption through her doctor's auspices, gives birth to a defective or mixed race child, the consequences can be horrendous. For in independent adoptions, plans are made long before the baby's birth for the immediate placement of the newborn infant with a chosen couple. The adopting parents, often alerted when the mother enters the hospital, await delivery as if they themselves were in labor. When the infant is born with a handicap, the adopters, prepared as they are for the perfect child, can seldom accept a maimed one. The birth mother, suffering the self-imposed punishment of giving birth to a "freak," is confronted with the fact that not only does no one want her but no one wants her baby either.

The doctor knows just what to do. Belatedly he calls the adoption agency and asks that it send someone, to come immediately, today, this afternoon and take the baby away. The whole process, so indifferent to human sensitivity, is gross and ugly. An agency worker could have soothed the mother, taken the baby into foster care and given the mother time for recovery and thoughtful decision-making. An agency would have located proper parents for the child and allowed time for the emotional storm to blow over. Adoptive parents would not thus be thrust into the position of having to turn down a child, about which they might suffer unnecessary guilt. The difference between birth parents, who must accept their handicapped children, and adopters free to make a choice is clearly illustrated by such cases.

Because a family with both a mother and a father is preferable to a single parent home, unmarried persons who want to adopt usually have to consider children for whom there are no adopting couples, the hard-to-place children. Although many adoptees with medical problems cannot be properly cared for by single parents, older children and those of mixed race are frequently adopted by single persons both male and female.

In single parent adoptions, the larger family group (the grandparents, aunts, uncles, etc.) is an especially important part of the life of the adopted child. It is there that the child will find his surrogate father or mother. Thus in considering applications from single parents, the adoption agency must investigate the family clan as well.

Racial integration in the 1960s opened the opportunity for closer relationship between blacks and whites, resulting in a marked increase in mixed race babies. Almost all these babies were born of white mothers and black fathers. In only one case in my experience, was the reverse true. That mother, like most black mothers, kept her baby after all. Most white mothers who gave birth to mulatto babies could not consider taking their babies home to their parents. White parents were more appalled by having dusky grandchildren than by their daughters' pregnancies, rationalizing that their daughters were victims of rather than participants in the sex act. Black middle-class parents tended to be greater censors of their pregnant daughters, but no matter what they thought of the young mothers, more often than not, they would take their illegitimate grandchildren home.

Many young white mothers, not biased when it came to their black lovers, preferred that their mixed race babies be adopted by white couples. To the black population a black-white child is black and should be in a black home. But to the white mother, the child is half white and belongs in a family like her own.

Most of the mixed race babies were adopted by young white couples and occasionally by black parents who found the babies' light complexions appealing. In a few instances I was fortunate in being able to place a mixed race baby with a mixed race couple.

In the civil rights decade of the sixties, liberal white adopters considered adoption of a black or half-black baby to be appropriate and in tune with the times. But strong objections were raised by black social workers. They expressed the conviction that such adoptions were motivated by humanitarian sentimentality and that no white parents could comprehend or teach black children how to deal with the prejudices they would face. They saw the children as black vassals in a white environment. True as the dire prediction of the black social workers may prove to be, the options open to the agencies were limited. Few black couples came forth to adopt the vast number of black and mulatto babies. Even as we foresaw that black children in white American homes were bound to face unique difficulties, there were no better alternatives.

Some of these mixed race children were placed overseas in Scandinavian homes, where even with the extreme contrast between the light parents and the dark children, color is not a factor for prejudice. In removing black children from an environment where they would be taught defenses against white bias, they would instead be raised in homes tolerant of all racial differences. We can only hope that these displaced children will find a new way of dealing with both white and black prejudices.

In this country, transracial adoption of Oriental children is more acceptable for white parents than is their adoption of black children. Adoption of children from the orphanages of Asia, though complicated by delay and bureaucratic regulations, is oversubscribed, whereas black children available here still wait for adoptive homes.

Some American couples asked specifically for Vietnamese children as a way of expressing atonement for our military involvement in that country. But most white adopters were not particular from which country their Asian children came. Between Korea and the United States a workable system of intercountry adoptions was developed. But for the adoption of other Asian children, the bureaucratic tangle was late in unraveling. Servicemen and other Americans living in Vietnam were more successful in adopting Vietnamese orphans when they were on hand to pressure the authorities and to see that birth records, medical clearances, exit permits, passports, visas, etc. were in order.

One can commiserate with a Korean child, flown in one day's time from the community of an orphanage, where an enormous family of playmates speaks a familiar tongue, to a strange nuclear family in suburban America, where nothing, not even the language, is linked to his past life. The change from a meagre Far Eastern diet of rice to an abundant fare of meat and potatoes is one of the most trying and persistent adjustments for both children and parents.

Whether children are physiologically geared for certain foods, or psychologically cling to a nostalgic taste is hard to tell. Children adopted from abroad are usually several years old and may have already established a palate for black beans or brown rice. But what of the Japanese girl, adopted by Americans in Japan and raised by them from babyhood, who, now 16, has a craving, almost an addiction for rice?

The one advantage in the adoption of older children, either native or foreign, is that no fiction about their adoption is possible. There can be no secrecy in the fact of adoption, no whispered words behind closed doors, no pretense. Nothing is withheld. Children adopted at age three or over, though they may repress them, have memories of another life. Their parents are, perforce, more candid and open about adoption. Parents adopting older American children are tested and challenged, but their problems do not compare to the couples who adopt children whose language, customs and backgrounds are utterly foreign. Parents adopting older children from abroad must be prepared for a six-month culture shock in their children. One example will illustrate a typical experience in the adjustment of those displaced adoptees.

Theresa and her four siblings had been housed in orphanages since she was one year old, when her overburdened mother could no longer support them. Theresa was eight, the only one of the family not yet adopted, when she was discovered by a prospective American adopter in a Central American orphanage. She was considered unadoptable because of advanced age. The American mother was convinced this girl was meant for her and took Theresa to her hotel, awaiting the adoption through the local court. Adoption into a family from the United States was carefully explained to Theresa by her social worker, and she apparently had no qualms about a trip to a new land and a new family. In ten days the adoption was authorized and mother and daughter flew to the U.S. and joined the other family members.

All was peaceful for two days as Theresa was introduced to a bed of her own, to dolls and toys such as she had never known. Then, like a bolt out of the blue, Theresa erupted. After an hour's bath she refused to get out of the tub. Her mother drained the tub, Theresa filled it, mother drained, Theresa filled, drained, filled until her mother lifted her bodily from the tub.

In her room she kicked, screamed and resisted being dressed. Ordinarily a neat child, she pulled her clothes from the drawer, the bedclothes from the bed. She threw lamps out the window, all the while screaming in Spanish without interruption. She allowed no one to touch her, kicked her mother away, ran outdoors and back in again, and banging her head against the wall called "mama, mama" in an hysterical tirade. This went on for almost three hours. The desperate parents finally recalled that Theresa loved music and left her in her room with the record player turned on to pastoral strains. Shortly, Theresa joined her parents as if nothing had happened.

Four days later the next confrontation started. On the way to the grocery store Theresa insisted on unlocking the car doors, and in the store she screamed her demands for grocery items, stamped her feet and finally refused to get back in the car. Left behind, she ran after the car, and on being taken in, was utterly peaceful and without residual anger.

In other episodes Theresa demanded that her shoes be brought to her and that she be dressed by her mother. On one occasion, she packed her bag to run away. She seemed to be insatiable in her need for attention and for testing her parents' tolerance and love. She needed a lot of reassurance to alleviate her fears. She feared loss of her mother and, at times of insecurity, clung doggedly to her mother's legs. She resisted family members going out, fearing they would not return. When family friends visited on their way to Central America, she was terrified that she was to be taken back to the orphanage by them. As time passed these outbursts of frustration became less frequent and intense.

In seeking to understand Theresa's behavior, her parents found it helpful to imagine themselves in her place, which was easier for the mother who had seen the orphanage where Theresa had lived. They learned that spanking, associated with the beatings in her babyhood, produced only negative results. They recognized that Theresa's sleeplessness was due to fear associated with the novel experience of being in bed alone. A Raggedy Ann doll as big as she was cured her insomnia. They saw that she cherished her possessions and feared they would be stolen from her, so they allowed her to keep her new bicycle in her upstairs bedroom.

From a child who would allow no one to touch her, Theresa became, in one year, a spontaneous and affectionate girl. She learned English very quickly and proved to be a bright and eager student. It took a year of reassurance in her new home before Theresa confessed that she thought that she had been adopted to be a servant. Her emerging personality revealed a sensitive human being with poise, strength and a sense of humor. Though at one point the parents wondered what they had let themselves in for, and, in desperation, whether there was any way out, they were gratified that both they and Theresa had survived and had come through the ordeal with mutual respect and love.

There is an increasing number of young families who have adopted children as well as birth children. Many of the adoptees are of the hard-to-place minorities. Conscientious young parents express their concern about the population explosion by planning to have one child and adopt the others. They take for granted that adoption is available to them and that adopted children will hold an equal place in the family with the birth children. The likelihood of their adopting children today is remote, but if they are successful it is probable that they will not treat their birth and adopted children differently. An individual parent may be inherently attuned to one or another child, whose personality sparks something in himself, but that special child could well be the adopted one.

Sibling rivalry in mixed families may focus on competition between the adopted children and birth children for the attention of their parents or their relative value in the family. A few adopters, feeling less secure in relationship to the adopted children, or perhaps because of greater sympathy for them, will favor the adopted over the birth children. I have noted however that it is grandparents rather than parents who show favoritism, and usually to the birth grandchildren. One birth child, puzzled by the *equal* treatment given him and his adopted siblings, asked, "Do you love me the same or do you love me more?"

For many adopters the first child will always be special. In their excitement about the long awaited child they may be blindly ecstatic about him, and find themselves dubious that the second child, whether born to them or adopted, could ever measure up. Some parents, for this reason, never adopt a second time. On the other hand, parents who have some reservations about adoption itself are more confident in loving the second child, as they have found how much they have come to love the first.

It seldom occurs to parents of mixed families to think which of their children were adopted and which were born to them. Whether they are adopted into the family or born into it, children somehow manage to win their own way into the hearts of their waiting parents.

<table>
<tr><td>

14
</td><td>

OPENING PANDORA'S BOX
</td></tr>
</table>

MR. AND MRS. MEYER HAD ALWAYS prided themselves on their children's lack of interest in adoption. Their adopted children had asked no questions and in fact had turned their parents off when the subject of adoption was raised. The Meyers felt they had proved by their experience that being adopted was truly no different than being born into a family.

The Meyers' fast-paced living did not lend itself to probing the unseen. They were a family of activists, all except for one member, their twenty-two-year-old daughter, Rebecca. She was sensitive and reserved, watching rather than partaking in family disputes. Rebecca's thoughtfulness for the feelings of others had always pleased her parents. She had never caused them a moment's worry. She was spoken of as "the mature one."

Growing up and going off to college, she had kept her family in touch with her daily doings, had brought her friends home for vacations and given her parents no cause for concern. Her announced engagement was, to her parents, the culmination of a delightful, carefree childhood and youth. Busily occupied with wedding plans, they were astounded and crushed when Rebecca, the mature one, broke her engagement without explanation and became deeply depressed.

Rebecca seemed to them a different person, angry, irrational and uncommunicative. She could not be reached by her pleading mother or her reprimanding father. It was to her older brother that she finally turned in tears of anguish.

"I don't belong anywhere," she sobbed. "Dad and Mom never understood how I needed to know. Who am I anyway? I didn't just begin twenty-two years ago. The folks have been so good to me I wouldn't want to hurt them. They wouldn't believe how much I have thought about my other family all these years. Being engaged made me realize how little I knew. What could I bring to a marriage and to children? Nothing, just a blank page for a family heritage.

Here I am with my whole life ahead of me, but my past is an empty void. I can never make them understand."

How do adoptive parents regard the prospect of their children's search and reunion with birth mothers? I asked this question of all the parents I interviewed. The majority of adopters felt that the search would be like opening Pandora's box but none of them denied the *right* of the grown adoptees to search. A few were ready to assist their children in finding birth mothers by locating original documents and records, and even by petitioning the court. But many others viewed reunion as destructive to their children's wellbeing and said they would either oppose or discourage it. They saw reunion with birth parents as the first step in the imposition of emotional pressure on their children. "Why upset the apple cart?" they said, "There is no sense in digging up the past."

Parents of young children at ages of greatest dependency were generally more resistant to the idea of their children's eventual contact with birth mothers than were parents of older children approaching adulthood. Young adopters could not foresee that the possessiveness that they were experiencing as new parents would change as their children grew and no longer needed or sought their protection.

Most adopters, unfortunately, are convinced that their children's interest in finding birth parents is evidence of their own failure as parents. As one mother said, "If my children looked for their other mothers, that would be against me." One couple I have heard of was so hurt and angered by their son's meeting with his birth mother that they suggested he could call them, his adopted parents, Mr. and Mrs. since he now had another mother and father.

In talking about their children's reunions with birth parents, adopters revealed much about themselves. One mother with feelings of inadequacy was fearful that the birth mother would be deeply loved and would replace her. Another was able to accept reunion for her problem son but not for her dutiful daughter. A reserved adoptive mother thought the birth mother had a right to be left alone, regardless of her offspring's desire.

A mother of means feared the emotional pressure a rediscovered birth mother might impose on her child who, through guilt or pity, would be forever burdened with her birth mother's financial support.

Another mother reasoned, "Since neither birth nor adopted children can choose what kind of family they are to be raised in, why should adopted children have the right of choice between two families?" One forthright mother felt the adoptee's search was an ego trip, an unhealthy dwelling on self. She would discourage her children from speculating on their origins and encourage their turning outward to a life of activity and service. Several mothers, who thought in traditional ways about the questionable reputation of unmarried mothers, feared that their children would learn sordid facts that would be detrimental to their self-images.

One mother, particularly sensitive to the feelings of others, feared that the birth mother's reunion with her once abandoned child would renew her feelings of guilt. Another feared that her child would feel rejected a second time. A mother who was caught up in the throes of her adopted daughter's rebellious adolescence feared she would be blamed by the birth mother for her child's unhappiness in adoption.

A divorced adoptive mother felt the birth mother would be unnecessarily upset by the failure of the adopters to provide the two-parent family she had anticipated for her child in adoption. One mother who knew that the birth parents had planned to marry after surrendering their infant for adoption feared that they would impose a double threat to the unity of the adoptive family.

Grateful as the adopters were to birth parents for the gift of children, they did not wish the children to receive gifts of money or inheritance from the birth parents. Adopted adults who at one time had been interested in searching their own records or contacting their birth parents seemed to turn around completely, eschewing such interest, when they themselves became adoptive parents and were faced with a similar curiosity in their children. Most Mormon parents, in spite of their abiding concern for "ancestors behind the veil" did not regard their adopted children's true ancestry differently than other adopters.

A few adoptive parents whom I interviewed believed that an adoptee's desire for reunion with birth parents was understandable and acceptable. They did not think a reunion would threaten their established relationship or that it would be harmful for their adult children to seek and find their birth parents. As one mother said, "I want to be the only mother, but if my daughter really feels the need to find her other mother, I will help her." Another mother pictured herself in her daughter's place and knew that she would want to find her birth mother if she were adopted. She anticipated her daughter's search without misgivings. Several parents were so delighted with their adopted children that they were convinced the birth parents must be equally attractive. They hoped some day to know their children's first parents.

One adoptive couple went a step further. They believed that all adopted persons needed to reconstitute themselves as adults in their own hereditary relationships, that only through thorough knowledge of their backgrounds, including contact with birth families, would their children become psychologically whole. To this couple, the issue was not whether the search for birth mothers should be made, but how it could best be conducted. They were convinced that the true facts of origin would be much easier for their children to deal with, whether pleasant or unsavory, than the doubt and uncertainty of the unknown. If their children's backgrounds proved to be criminal or degenerate, they would give their children additional support to overcome the blow. Removing the block to concealed heritage they felt, would, enable their children to function freely and at their best. They hoped that by the time their children were adults all records would be open to them merely for the asking.

My experience does not speak for all young adoptees, but those I interviewed, between the ages of 14 and 20, seemed satisfied with the status quo. I saw no evidence of anger at birth parents or regret in being adopted. All of them had a good deal of information on their birth heritage already. They were indifferent to the idea of searching their records and quite put out by the thought of reunion with their birth parents. They expressed interest in knowing more about themselves but were not motivated to seek information actively. Several asked if I had known their first mothers and were interested in my descriptions of their birth parents and the reasons they surrendered their children for adoption. One adolescent, who was born with a physical defect, sought assurance that his birth mother was not similarly afflicted by asking several times about her health.

Since the search for birth parents requires strong motivation, it normally comes to adoptees, if at all, in adulthood. However, young children may fantasize the search and reunion without specific direction or plan.

The search may actually begin in childhood with an occurrence, common to many families, of children threatening to leave home. In the adoptive family, the angry child packing his bag has an added dimension. He is not only threatening to leave home but is threatening to find his other parents as well. The search in childhood may never be renewed or it may be a precursor of events to come. One adoptive mother told me of her experience with her son Colin.

Colin, who was seven, had been watching his mother cuddling his baby sister until he could stand it no longer. He was jealous of the attention his sister got and angry at his mother for not heeding his demands. He hit his sister and was sent to his room to think about his misbehavior.

After a period of quiet, Colin opened the door of his room and yelled into the empty hallway, "Everyone in this house hates me but you won't have to see me around much longer." The mother ignored his cry for attention and Colin tried again. "I'm going to pack up all my things and take off." Again silence, so Colin yelled louder, "You hate me but I know someone who thinks I'm all right. I'm going to find her. I'm going to look for my real mother."

To this threat his mother responded. Coming to his room she tried to reason with Colin. She protested that she did love him and always would. She tried to persuade Colin to wait and talk it over with his father. She explained that he could not find his first mother anyway since no one knew where she lived.

Colin, unconsoled, declared, "I hate everyone in this house. I'm going." Scared and uncertain, Colin's mother held herself in check and, remembering how her own mother had handled her departure from home as a child, she helped him pack his bag and opened the door for him. Fearfully she watched him from the window, a lone little figure walking away from her. She burst into tears.

Her tears were soon dried for in a few minutes she saw her adored young son come trundling back, a little shame-faced but smiling. He looked up as she opened the door, "Gee Mom, I think I'll wait until after supper. I'm awfully hungry."

Parents of young adopted children, fearful of the prospect of their search for birth mothers, can sit back and relax. They will probably be grandparents before they are confronted with the possibility. I wish all adoptive parents could embrace the views of one mature and wise adoptive mother. She said, "I expect to share my daughter's love with her husband when she marries. If she finds and comes to love her first mother I can share that too. Love is not a limited quality."

15 SOCIAL WORKERS REGARD THE SEARCH

I WAS ONCE CONFRONTED BY A GIRL of eighteen searching her heritage in the agency files. She had been placed for adoption before my time and I didn't know her background. Her adoptive family had promised that when she reached eighteen they would take her back to the agency to get the information about herself which they had not been given. The whole family came to Washington for the great event. While her mother and siblings wandered through the Smithsonian museums, Amy and her father came to the agency.

As executive director, I was authorized by adoption regulation to read the record and reveal the contents if, in my opinion, it served the "best interests of the child."

The record contained detailed descriptions of both the birth mother's and father's families. It described the parents' relationship, their thinking, their plans, and their final decision to place Amy in adoption. It was a story typical of an out-of-wedlock pregnancy: the naive and lonely young girl falling in love with a more sophisticated young man, the couples' sexual compatability not accompanied by mutual interests, the unexpected pregnancy clarifying their relationship as transitory.

There was one unusual feature in the recorded account. The birth father had seriously considered keeping the baby himself. He had shown himself to be responsible, standing by the birth mother, paying for her support and medical costs. He showed concern for his child's welfare. This fact came as a revelation to Amy. She had never given much thought to her birth father. She now saw him, as she did her adoptive father, as a sensitive and caring person.

Her father observed her interest with satisfaction, leaving it to her to question me. It was obvious to both of us that Amy's appearance and her modest, thoughtful disposition were a true replica of her birth mother as described in the record.

As the story of her family background came forth bit by bit from the agency record, Amy was engrossed by the details. Experienced as I was in many similar cases, I was able to reconstruct the circumstances which led to Amy's surrender for adoption. Whatever blame she may have felt toward her birth mother was dispelled.

Two disclosures had immediate significance for Amy. The first was that everyone involved in plans for her life the social workers, her birth mother, and especially her birth father—had cared about her. The second revelation was that, rather than being a dark-eyed Italian as she had always assumed, she was of German descent. Amy's pleasure in hearing the story of her birth and her first parents was written on her glowing countenance.

As she left with her father, I asked Amy if she thought she would search further for her parents. "I don't think I need to anymore," she replied.

— — — — — — — — — —

Social workers look upon the movement to open sealed records as destructive of the institution of adoption. Adoption agencies have always regarded their records as inviolate, and claim discretionary power to withhold information contained in them. On the other hand, public documents related to adoption in courts and bureaus of vital records were open until the early forties. Curious and malevolent strangers could peruse them at will. The unfortunate consequences for the adopted child and his family led to the sealing of public records in one state after another. Today only in the state of Kansas can adult adoptees obtain on request their original birth certificates containing the names of their birth parents. The laws in Alabama and Virginia allow adult adoptees access to official records but experience shows that clerks in the bureaus of vital records in these states often question, delay and discourage such requests.

The original intent of the closed records was to protect the adopted child from public scrutiny. Long experience with children disrupted by change in and out of foster and parental homes has convinced social workers of the benefit for children of one permanent family. Hence adoption. Social workers who know the locations of both birth and adoptive parents have conscientiously preserved the integrity of the adoptive home in keeping the two sets of parents separated. The identity of the adopters is not known by the birth parents or they by the adopters. The closed records insured the child's separation from birth parents so that he could be brought up by his adopters without harassment.

It is a move which no doubt benefited most adopted children. However the original intent has been lost and distorted. The adopted child grown to adulthood and no longer needing the earlier safeguards finds that when he requests his birth certificate the record has been permanently hidden in a bureaucratic labyrinth. The protection meant for the child has become a shield behind which adoptive parents may deny their adoptee's heritage without fear of disclosure. Social workers see the barrier as protecting all three parties to adoption, as well as safeguarding their own records of placements. Closed records have supported adoption as we know it today.

Sealed records also shield the birth mother from public scrutiny. All employees in hospitals, record rooms, the bureaus of vital records, as well as the social agencies are directed to protect from disclosure the identity of a woman having a child out of wedlock or even of a married woman who is giving up her baby for adoption. Hospital personnel may even go along with a fiction of infant death to protect the mother's plan for adoption of the baby. The unmarried mother is shielded from the shame of the Scarlet Letter, which is rather quickly fading into pale pink.

The relationship between the social worker and the client is often compared to that of the doctor and patient or the priest and confessor. Confidentiality is a tenet of the social worker's code of ethics. The opening of adoption records cuts into the very heart of the social agencies' doctrine of confidentiality. Whether or not social workers actually promise secrecy to their clients, confidentiality is assumed.

As recipients of confessions given in private the adoption agencies feel they are the only ones in a position to judge what information may be revealed and to whom. In their protective role they even resist opening records to the court.

The promise of confidentiality has allowed social workers in the past to elicit valuable information from reluctant clients, especially alleged fathers who are alarmed that their identities may be disclosed. Unmarried mothers have named their parents and other members of their families in trust that the social worker will keep her knowledge of the pregnancy from them. To the social worker, a trust once given an unmarried mother must always be honored. Secrecy in the practice of adoption has been so well rooted that the merit of absolute confidentiality for all time has been taken for granted.

Most social agencies have no problem with applying this principle. Only in adoption agencies, where the needs of the grown adoptee impinge upon the trust of secrecy given to his birth parents, does confusion arise. With the increasing demand by grown adoptees to know where they came from, adoption workers have been forced to reexamine the bases for confidentiality. They have also had to modify former thinking in view of the changing moral climate today.

Do we promise secrecy to the grave? At the time assurances of confidentiality are given, the unmarried mother is usually a young woman fearful for her reputation. The adopting parents are fearful too of losing their child to her. Thirty years later, when an adoptee may be searching out his origins, the unmarried mother is a mature woman in her fifties and the adoptive parents have already launched their child into an independent life. The original basis for secrecy appears less relevant as time passes.

Unlike psychiatrists who seem able to counsel patients with minimal recording, social workers generally describe their interviews with unmarried mothers in great detail. Hundreds of files of painstakingly recorded cases are sealed away in the basements of adoption agencies. What are the records for? Who are they for? The birth parents, the adoptive parents, or the adoptee?

Do situations exist which make confidentiality of adoption records absurd? What about the expectant mother, herself adopted at infancy and now distraught by the specter of an inherited disorder in her unborn child? What about the youth who suspects that his fiancee is his natural sister? What about the woman of seventy who seeks her family name in the dusty files of the Washington Home for Foundlings?

Adoption agencies have had to compromise. While withholding data which would identify birth parents by name, many are now willing to give adopted adults accounts which they once considered confidential. They are conscience-stricken though, for much of the information they disclose may originally have been given in secrecy. The social worker's ultimate fear is that the background history will not suffice, and the adult adoptee will pursue the search until he finds his birth mother.

This is not often the case. Evidence suggests that the adopted persons who are most persistent in their searches for their birth parents are those who have been given no information about them, or whose adoptions have been hidden from them. They apparently feel that only by meeting their birth parents in person can they learn the truth about themselves.

Social workers are also worried that if records are opened there will be a multitude of requests. Evidence does not bear this out either. In Scotland, where birth records are open, the number of adopted persons seeking their birth certificates is minuscule. In the three states of this country where records are open to adult adoptees, the number of requests are insignificant and easily handled. And in states where records are sealed, directors of bureaus of vital records are often distressed by having to turn down pleading adoptees seeking identity.

Adopted persons are often victimized by the extremes to which the concern for confidentiality is carried. To preserve confidentiality, records of unmarried mothers who had lived in a maternity home in Washington were burned so that the "wrong parties" would not get hold of them. A forty-year-old adoption record in the files of a Washington adoption agency was destroyed when an adoptee claimed inheritance from his adoptive parents and needed proof contained in the record. In contrast, the Columbia Hospital for Women in Washington has preserved on microfilm all records of illegitimate births at the hospital since 1865.

There is danger that agencies, anticipating the opening of records, will destroy them on the pretext of sparing the feelings of the adopted persons who search for them. Social workers argue that although some adoption records are acceptable and might be shared with adoptees, others reveal backgrounds which would be destructive to them. But to an adoptee, the denial of access to his birth certificate and adoption record can be more crushing than the story they tell. A grown adoptee learning of a dubious heritage might be thankful to know that his adoption had spared him from a destructive birthright. There is evidence that adopted adults are relieved to know the facts of their beginnings, even when the revelations are distasteful. Unlike many children who live with it, degeneracy in their birth families would not have been experienced by the adoptees, merely perceived.

When agencies refuse to give information, the only recourse for the adoptee is the court where his adoption was finalized. If the court record is too brief to be satisfactory, the court may subpoena the agency's record for further illumination. Such was the case with Helen.

Helen was an adopted woman who had married young and given birth to a defective child. Her daughter's problem was thought to be genetic in origin. Divorced and increasingly troubled by her daughter's development, Helen sought information about her birth parents in order to shed light on her daughter's condition. She hired a lawyer who asked that the court record be opened. The court found "good cause" because of the child's physical impairment. When the court's record was found without medical data, information was requested of the adoption agency. They submitted only a partial report. The agency felt their record was too unpleasant to share completely.

Helen wrote about the agency's denial of her request in a letter to her lawyer. "I realize people think they are protecting me by not telling me the truth, but what they don't realize is that, not knowing is worse than knowing. I have all those fantasies about the worst. I imagine incest, murder, rape. Even if it is any of those extremes, I feel I am mature enough emotionally to handle the facts whatever they are."

Thinking about the agency's actions further, she became angry. She wrote, "How dare the agency play games with me. They seem to think that I am some kind of nut, that I would go around broadcasting my family's past. I have no intention of hurting anyone and I feel I have the common sense to handle the situation properly. They have made such a big deal out of this, it makes me want to know that much more."

Inconsistencies in the agency's partial report resulted in the entire file being subpoenaed by the court. Only then did Helen learn the whole story.

She learned that her mother was the only survivor of four children, two of whom had been stillborn. Her mother had congenital syphilis, was an alcoholic and psychotic. She had been hospitalized for dementia praecox both before and after Helen's birth. Helen's father was not identified.

Helen had three older half-siblings, two of whom were retarded. All three were brought up in institutions and foster homes.

As for herself, Helen learned that she was born prematurely and her early development was slow. In view of her history, adoption was not advocated, and for most of her first four years she had been in public care in hospitals and foster homes. When she was three, Helen was released by her mother to the Commissioner of Welfare, and, after another year in foster care, she was found suitable for adoption. She was adopted at the age of four years and four months.

In appreciation for the efforts of the court in obtaining the agency record, Helen wrote to the judge. "I found it most rewarding and beautifully written. The agency should be commended for the dedication and thoroughness of my files. My only feeling regarding my past is one of much gratitude because I was given the chance to have a decent life. I'm only sorry that my biological mother seemingly never had this offered to her as a child. She had a tragic start and more than likely a tragic end to her life. I hold no bitterness, just compassion for a very sick woman. I pray that, somehow, my half-sister eventually found a chance for a good life. I was disappointed that there doesn't seem to be any connection medically with my daughter's illness. I guess from here on her destiny lies in God's hands."

With the full knowledge of her heritage Helen was more certain about what her future plans would be. Because of her family history she was determined to bring no more children into the world, although with her new self-confidence, she remarried after ten years as a single woman.

The strongest argument social workers raise against the search is the shock a birth mother may suffer from confrontation with an offspring, long buried in her past. Probably she will have married and had other children. She may have established a conforming way of life for herself, separate from and incompatible with her youthful transgression. She may have kept the secret from her husband.

Contrary to public surmise, birth mothers' repudiation of their returning offspring is exceptional. A birth mother may live on two levels of consciousness, one in her life with children of recent years and the other in flashes from the past of a child she surrendered for adoption. Confronted by reunion, mothers are likely to be more emotionally touched than their returning offspring. Their guilt in having surrendered their infants is eased, and they may even attempt to make up for lost years of mothering. A mother's acceptance of the ghost from the past depends upon the manner of her adult life, enabling her in some cases to incorporate the stranger into it. If the renewed relationship between the two adults proves inharmonious, there need be no obligation on either side to sustain it.

Although social workers think primarily in terms of protecting birth mothers from being found by their adult offspring, there are an increasing number of mothers who shun protection, who are themselves engaged in the search. Their search lacks the justification which that of the adopted person possesses. It is understandable on an emotional level but as a civil rights issue such a search is not well grounded. The prior relinquishment of parental rights made voluntarily is forever binding.

The social worker who once looked upon the dependent child as a defenseless individual for whose protection she labored no longer recognizes him when he is grown. Faced with the adoptee as an adult she finds her orientation dislodged. The child placed in adoption was supposed to live happily ever after. Consequently the social worker assumes that the adoptee's search is based on orneriness. Viewing it as a personal indictment, she may resent his ingratitude for the adoption which had been so thoughtfully arranged.

For the adoptee the search which began in curiosity may well end in anger, not at the birth parents who gave him up, but at the social worker and other authorized persons who deny him access to his records.

Adoption agencies have lost their way. They have confused their priorities when they honor the desires of the adoptive parents and the confidentiality granted birth parents ahead of the needs of the adopted individual. The principal client of the past is still the principal client in the present. He is the only one of the three parties to adoption who had no voice in the arrangements for his adoption. He signed no document. He pledged no secrecy. Can the grown adoptee morally be denied the record of his beginnings, including the names of his birth parents?

Agencies must be prepared for the day which will surely come when records will be legally opened to adopted adults on request. Are they equipped to deal with it? Can they welcome the returning adoptee to whom they gave their first loyalty in years gone by? When he comes back, the social worker must be ready to grant to him the same first loyalty as before, and provide a final service in answer to his question, "Who am I?".

THE
ADULT
ADOPTEES
SEEK
IDENTITY

CONSTANCE WAS BORN IN THE DISTRICT of Columbia. She had been delivered at the Florence Crittenden Home and placed for adoption at two months of age. She was raised as an only child by anxious and adoring parents. Although Constance felt she never really belonged in her adoptive home, the years passed peacefully enough in a safe and conventional way. When Constance was twenty-eight she married and had her first child as she turned thirty. Her pregnancy disturbed her. Thoughts that her child might carry defective traits obsessed her. Her interest in hereditary diseases, though previously of only passing concern, became an anxious fixation. At times she knew her fears to be irrational, yet in moments of panic she could not be reassured. Might she be a carrier of multiple sclerosis or Huntington's disease? Who could tell her it was not so? The limitations of adoption suddenly became real to her. Her unborn child could have no more than half a heritage. Cut off as she was from her own lineage, she had no ancestry to bestow upon her own offspring. She determined to search for her mother and learn about herself.

Her first move was successful. She found her name. A birth certificate for December 10 at the Bureau of Vital Records was the only one recorded on that day from the small maternity home facility where she was born. She was lucky. If she had been born three years later, the original record of her birth would have been unavailable to her, sealed into a closed file. She saw her mother's name, her own name, but no name for her father or home address.

Constance made an appointment at the maternity home where she had been born, explaining her interest in finding out what they knew about her mother and the circumstances of her birth. An understanding social worker located the record through the maiden name of her mother on her birth certificate. She was reassured that her mother's medical history was flawless. The social worker refused to let her read the record itself, explaining the need to protect the mother, and cautioned her to pursue the matter no further. Constance was incensed that only short excerpts of the very long record were read aloud to her. She felt she was being treated like a teenage resident of the maternity home, not a grown woman with a serious interest in her heritage.

Her next appointment was at the office of the adoption agency which had placed her. From the factual material read to her by the social worker, she found her mother's employment listed as "newspaperwoman." Constance was again advised to drop the search for the sake of her adoptive parents as well as for her birth mother.

From this point on in her search, Constance did not reveal her relationship to the person she sought, but posed as a genealogist tracing her family line. Although some persons regarded her youthful interest in genealogy with skepticism, her quest was generally accepted at face value.

There were four newspapers in Washington at the time of her birth. Constance checked them all. Dogged and persistent, she finally located a reporter who remembered her mother though he did not know much about her. He told Constance she had left quite suddenly after a short period of employment. Through his efforts, old personnel files were unearthed, and in one of them Constance found her mother's name and Washington address. Nervously anticipating whom she would find, she went to the address. The woman who answered the door did not know her mother. She suggested Constance talk to a neighbor who had lived there for years.

The neighbor recalled a friendly young girl (who, she said, looked a lot like Constance) who left to get married shortly after her fiance returned from the war in Europe. "I think he was an aviator but I don't believe I ever heard his name," she said, trying to remember. Constance was discouraged as she left. She had come so close to her mother but still knew so little. She had learned only that her mother had come from a western state, probably Colorado, and that she had left Washington around March of 1943 to be married.

Disheartened, Constance was about to give up the search. A chance meeting with another adopted adult who had encountered similar obstacles gave her new strength. She suggested that the mother might have gone home to be married and her marriage would be recorded in the bureau of records in the State of Colorado.

Constance went to Colorado. She had only to search through a month of recorded marriages when her mother's maiden name leaped to her from the page. She found her mother's married name and the town where her family had lived. In the town's library Constance met an older woman who had known the family and who located the address and phone number of her mother through friends. She was alive and living in Oregon. The end of the search was in sight, the possibility of reunion was real. The moment of decision had arrived.

Only now did Constance hesitate, old fears of rejection overcoming her usual self-confidence. Would her mother believe her? Would she acknowledge her? What would she be like? What would her husband think if he didn't know about the baby? Would she find she had half-sisters and brothers? Maybe she should drop the whole thing.

The warnings of the social workers came to mind. Was she really disturbed, as they implied, in wanting to see her mother face to face? Would she upset her mother in the new life she had made for herself? Would her mother deny the truth and turn her away? She debated all possibilities, but having gone so far she could not stop now.

She would not want to confront her mother unannounced. That would be unfair. A letter, even a registered one, might be opened by others. She decided to phone in the daytime when her mother might be home alone. If there were children, they would be in school.

She chose a day when the sun was out and she felt good about herself and positive about what she was about to do. With shaking body and pounding heart she asked the operator to dial for her. Making the long distance connection seemed to take forever. The phone rang several times and finally a woman's voice spoke. Was this the voice of her mother, the mother she had sought for so long—just a voice at the other end of a phone? Quaking and tense, she repeated the words she had practiced saying, "This is your daughter, born in 1943 in Washington."

A brusque defensive reply struck terror into Constance's heart. "I have no daughter of that description."

Drained and empty, Constance tried once more. "Didn't you work on a newspaper and live on R Street in Washington? Didn't you have a baby at Florence Crittendon Home and give her up for adoption? I have been looking for you for years. I am your daughter."

After what seemed to Constance an endless silence, the other voice finally replied, "Can it really be true? After all these years!"

———————————

Adopted adult is an expression so new in the language that, when hearing it for the first time, listeners are bewildered and ask, "What's that?" The mystification engendered by the expression demonstrates the void in our concept of adoption. Either an adopted child never grows up or he outgrows his adoption. He is expected to shed the consciousness of his adoption as he matures, abandoning self-speculation and rationalizing his unusual status as immaterial.

The assumption that the adult life of the adopted is untroubled by the fact of adoption is not true for many and perhaps for most adopted adults. Whereas the need of a known heritage for adopted persons used to be buried in self-consciousness and shame, adopted adults are now demanding to know where they came from and who are their natural forebears.

Some, of course, have no apparent desire or need to search. There may be psychological blocks which keep them from acknowledging interest in their birth heritage, or the idea of a search may simply not seem relevant to their lives. But for many others, the need to know can be a vital concern.

In some ways, the interest shown in the search for birth parents is related to the early curiosity of adopted children. The birth fathers, about whom few questions are asked by the children, are rarely sought by adult adoptees. Just as adopted girls ask more questions than boys, so the adopted adults who search are almost universally female. Perhaps men think it weak and unmanly to look for an unknown mother, but I suspect that women, as bearers of the next generation of children, are more intimately touched by pregnancy and birth than men. They more easily identify and want contact with the mothers who bore them.

Interest in the search for ancestry usually comes to an adopted woman after she has had a child. To a woman brought up in an adoptive family, the birth of her own baby is a deeply satisfying event. At last she has a blood kin. In giving birth she has also become like other people, a birth mother in a normal family. Looking for similarities between her child and herself awakens her to interest in her own heritage.

Most searching adopted adults state firmly that they are not looking for their mothers but trying to find themselves through their mothers. If agency records contained detailed background information and if it were available to them this material might suffice. However, many adoptees who know details of their backgrounds still seek the person of their birth mothers. The information is so important to them that receiving it second hand is not enough.

One adopted adult compared the plight of adoptees in search to that of amnesia victims. Both search for lost identities, yet society takes opposite attitudes toward them. Whereas the victim of amnesia receives public sympathy and every effort is made to open the door to his lost life, the adoptee is put down as a neurotic troublemaker, and the doors to his past are slammed in his face.

I have known a number of adopted adults who are active in the crusade for open records. Most of them are married women in their thirties with children of their own. They are generally intense, serious and dedicated. Some are angry and resentful, believing that adoption is an aberration which is never justifiable. Many seem to have a relationship more of duty than of love toward their adoptive parents. The great majority of adoptees, fearing to hurt their adoptive parents, have undertaken the search without their knowledge.

There are also individuals who, growing up contentedly in their adoptive homes, still wish to fill the blank spaces in their birth heritage. Some adoptees have searched and found their birth mothers with the encouragement and blessings of their parents.

At present the only legal way to obtain an adoption record is through a hearing before a judge in the court where the adoption took place, a location unknown to many adoptees. Petitioning the court on an individual basis is an expensive and prolonged process. So far, records have been opened only for good cause, such as a need for genetic information or to promote the psychological well-being of the adoptee. Curiosity is not considered sufficient cause.

Adopted adults feel that the desire to know the background information that comprises their heritages is itself good cause. Otherwise their constitutional rights are denied them. It flouts their guarantees of freedom of speech, their right to redress grievances, and due process, as well as the denial and disparagement of rights unspecified in the articles of the Bill of Rights. In addition, many adoptees feel they have been subjected to "involuntary servitude" prohibited in the Constitution. Yet, to date no judges have been willing to consider the issue on constitutional grounds.

Once undertaken, the process of search is so distressing that years may pass between the first request for a birth certificate and the final telephone call to the birth mother. Each new revelation must be absorbed by the adoptee and reconciled with his daily life before the next step in the search can be undertaken.

The search for self is approached with excitement, apprehension and a sense of wrongdoing. Each refusal by the bureau of vital statistics, the hospital record room, the doctor's office where the birth mother was a patient, and the adoption agency confirms the sense of inequity and increases the feeling of wrongdoing. Adopted adults working together against the rejections of officialdom have given individual adoptees the encouragement and strength to continue.

Adoptees are particularly sensitive to the feelings their birth mothers may have about being found. They respect a mother's wish to keep the past transgression a secret. They are not looking for further rejection. They are cautious in their approach and avoid disclosing their relationship to members of their mothers' current families. Only when the mothers themselves initiate disclosure of the long-held secret to their own families do adoptees feel free to reveal themselves. Most birth mothers willingly acknowledge to others their returning offspring. This is not surprising to me as I recall the many unmarried mothers who expressed hope that someday their children would find them.

The adoptee's search for the birth mother, which may have begun in anger at having been given up for adoption, seldom ends that way. Adoptee and mother meet in what one psychiatrist describes as "mutual forgiveness." The anger is easily displaced from the mother who surrendered them to the social worker who, they feel, must have forced the decision. The expressions "pressured into abandonment," "sold into slavery," and "stolen from their mothers" are commonly used by angry adoptees. They focus blame elsewhere to save themselves the pain of parental rejection.

The adopted adults who are raising the issue of the closed records are pioneers in a movement that has been long in surfacing. They explain their former reluctance to come into the open as solicitude for their adoptive parents. They feel obligated and grateful. One senses that parents and adoptees have not communicated in any depth, though they seem particularly sensitive to each other. The taboos of a lifetime prohibit the spoken words. Most adopted adults feel they are double-crossing their adopters when they search for their birth parents.

For twenty-five years, one woman, Jean Paton, has laced the country in her travels, attempting to awaken social workers, adoption agencies, and the public to the wrong done to adopted adults in keeping their records from them. She has observed that illegitimate, orphaned and adopted persons tend to be restless wanderers, always in search of the elusive nirvana. She has an extensive collection of books, which she feels confirms her theory. The adopted Henry Stanley wandered for a year in darkest Africa in search of the lost David Livingston. Miss Paton finds Stanley's famous first words to the missionary, "Dr. Livingston, I presume?" a typical example of the tentative, uncertain nature of many adopted persons. Writer Jack London, naturalist John Audubon, painter Paul Gauguin, and T. E. Lawrence of Arabia, all illegitimate, were restless travelers. Orphaned early in life were Baron Alexander von Humboldt, Sir Francis Drake, and Peter Freuchen; as were writers Rudyard Kipling, Herman Melville and Somerset Maugham.

The name of Miss Paton's organization, "Orphan Voyage," graphically pictures the plight of the adopted person searching the world for a lost identity.

An adopted adult herself, Jean Paton, at the age of forty, found her mother by locating her original birth certificate, a document not now available to adoptees in most states. She tells of her mother's joy in the reunion and her own satisfaction in filling the empty spaces in knowledge of herself. To her surprise, Jean found that beneath her previously serious and intense personality she had a sense of humor. She could laugh at herself for the first time in her life.

Far ahead of her time in her life's work, Miss Paton suffered the disdain and insult of a public unready for the concept of an adopted person's right to heritage. The hostility still exists. Many leaders in the search for open records use both their names, their birth names in their work for the cause and their given names in their married lives. By using their birth names, they protect their adoptive parents and families against the hostility that publicity of their cause arouses.

Despite hostility, Jean Paton's cause has flourished, especially since the emergence of Florence Fisher, a fiery character who has written and spoken with vehemence and unrelenting determination. Her organization in New York City, The Adoption Liberty

Movement, has been followed by others in most of the larger cities in the United States and Canada. Their names—Adoptees in Search, Link, Yesterday's Children—express the spirit and the purpose of their existence. Adopted adults are demanding rights to their original birth certificates, their hospital records, their histories from the agencies' files, and the court records of their adoptions. Some are searching for reunion with their birth parents.

It requires stealth and laborious detective work up blind alleys and behind closed doors for the adopted person to find his way. There may be an easier route: Adopted persons and their birth parents might register in a central file and be brought together in a truly matching process. Reunion files are set up in every organization run by adopted persons.

Reunions by registration are infrequent. In our mobile society only on a nationwide scale could a reunion file be truly effective. An adoptee's birth date alone would not be sufficient for identification in a country where so many adoptions have taken place. Additional data are needed, such as place of birth, hospital, agency, and the court where the adoption was finalized. The reunion file has the advantage of offering a channel for both parties in search. It gives birth parents the possibility of access to their adult offspring which they otherwise have no right to expect. Some adoptees believe the reunion file obscures the real issue they are fighting for: their right to know their birth parents even without their mothers' participation.

The search for family members lost to each other is well known to readers of two magazines published by the Tower Press Inc. in Seabrook, New Hampshire. In the section "Looking for Someone" of *Women's Circle* and in "Missing Persons" of *Household Hints,* blood relatives separated through adoption frequently seek each other.

One woman writes, "I am seeking my mother or family. My name is Minnie Ross or Rose. After birth I was placed in Baby Home near Portland, Oregon. Name on adoption papers is Mabel Lowden. My birth date: May 20, 1910." An answer to someone in search comes from Texas: "If Claude and Judy Ash will write me, I can give information about a child adopted out years ago." In Washington a ten-year-old adoptee whose mother subscribes to *Woman's Circle* is sure that someday she will find a letter from her birth mother in "Looking for Someone." One comes to feel that there is tenacity in blood relationships which is basic to humans, a tribal instinct as old as man.

There are some adopted adults who ardently believe that adoption is so abnormal and beset by insoluble problems that adoption should never be substituted for the natural relationship of a child with biological parents. I do not agree.

I am convinced that most adopted children are granted a fuller life through adoption by mature and loving adopters than they might have in the care of their usually youthful and often confused birth mothers. The problem is not adoption itself but rather the way in which social institutions and individual adopters handle the situation.

The institution of adoption has been based upon the premise that an adoptive family can be substituted for a biological one without noteworthy differences. To reinforce the theory that only the adopting family exists for the adoptee, concealment and distortion have been built into the system. In placing children with adopting families, adoption agencies minimize the biological parents and the facts of heritage; and adoptive parents in response to their own needs ignore or avoid recognizing their children's first parents. While they presume rejection by their biological parents, adoptees nevertheless identify with them. The sense of unworthiness which results may inhibit their growth, keeping them dependent and immature, abnormally grateful to their adopters and guilty in thoughts of disloyalty toward them.

This dire picture of adoption does not apply to all adopted persons and it need not apply to any. Simply by a release of the adoption records to all grown adoptees on demand the secrecy and concealment which distorts adoption today could be broken.

The courts, the agencies, the bureaus of vital records and the doctors who make independent placements are shielded by laws and regulations from having to disclose information which rightfully belongs to the adoptees. The requirement that an adoptee seeking to know where he came from show "good cause" in court or submit to "counseling" in an agency perpetuates his dependency on the will and judgment of others. He is treated differently from other adults who take for granted that their search for heritage is an absolute and irrefutable right. Granting the same civil right to adopted persons would not only release them from privation but alter adoption as it is now constituted.

The agencies, the courts, the doctors, and the adoptive parents, faced with the eventuality that facts formerly hidden will be revealed, will have to substitute candor for concealment and honesty for distortion. The effects will ripple backwards to free adoptees still in childhood from adult pretense. Adoptive parents will more readily face the fact that their adopted children are not their possessions, that they are born in one heritage, raised in another and will emerge as adults into the larger world which belongs equally to everyone.

AFTERWORD

In the past three years, the movement to open records to adult adoptees has had its ups and downs. While one state (Pennsylvania) opened its files for adoptees requesting their birth certificates, another (Montana) shut its away. At present legislation is pending in over a dozen states from New York to California. The hard work of educating legislators falls upon hundreds of persistent adoptees. It takes only a handful of legislators to seal the records again.

In spite of setbacks, there seems to be a growing sensitivity to adoptees' demand for a voice in adoption matters. In Maryland, a Governor's commission to study adoption laws included representatives from adoptee as well as birth parent organizations. On the federal level, a panel to formulate legislation for a model state adoption act also named one adoptee and one birth mother as participants. One section of the act recommends that adopted persons who have reached their majority be given copies of their original birth certificates, and their court records, on demand.

Preserving the birth mother's privacy has been the rationale for denying records to adult adoptees. But a number of birth parents have come out of hiding to join adopted persons in the movement to open adoption records; in 1976, they formed an organization, Concerned United Birthparents (CUB), which is now nationwide. In 1979, in Washington, D.C., CUB joined twenty-six adoptee groups from thirty-two states, Mexico, and Canada for the first American Adoption Conference. Adoptive parents, doctors, lawyers, and social workers attended as well. The conference ended with a resolution calling for adoption records, complete with identifying information, to be made available to all members of the adoption triad—birth parents, adoptive parents, and adoptees—at the adoptees' age of majority, or earlier if all members of the triad agree.

There are two other firsts in the movement for open records. One is the establishment of a nationwide registry for the uniting of separated relatives—SOUNDEX, a computerized system located in Carson City, Nevada. The other is the first case brought before the Supreme Court of the United States. The Adoptee Liberty Movement Association of New York and nineteen adopted adults, whose request for their records had been refused, are the plaintiffs. The defendants are adoption agencies, directors of bureaus of vital records, maternity hospitals, and judges. Although the court did not choose to review this case in 1980, others will surely follow until a judgment is made.

Meanwhile, in England, the 1975 Children's Act made adoption records available to adult adoptees on request, and it has not created the havoc anticipated by its opponents. The *New York Times* recently reported that the Department of Health and Social Services has issued a report to Parliament declaring that the opposition's fears were essentially unfounded. Furthermore, in the first year a mere one percent of adoptees took advantage of the opportunity, and of these only one in five expressed the intention of seeking out their birth parents.

The reunion between the adoptee and the birth mother may not be mutually gratifying. One problem can be the timing. The usual age for an adoptee to begin seeking his birth mother is thirty, whereas a mother who has decided to seek her child expects that at twenty-one he will be ready to meet her. She may be disappointed to find the young person resentful of the intrusion. An intermediary could forestall such painful moments.

An adopted adult seeking his birth mother, however, should realize that the introduction of an intermediary abrogates her right of privacy, a right she may wish to maintain. As long as no one else is involved, she can meet directly with her child and keep the relationship secret. It is significant that brothers and sisters serarated by adoption usually seek the less emotional reunions with each other before looking for their parents.

Leaders of adoptee and birth-parent groups have come to recognize the complexities of the emotional marriage of long separated parent and child. In recent months post-reunion groups have been formed to air the problems of these connected but disjointed relationships.

The ideal reunion is a meeting not only of an adoptee and his birth mother but of both families. Such treasured meetings do happen, but only when both the birth and the adoptive parents are mature enough to appreciate what each has contributed to the lives of the others, and especially what they have both given to the growth and well-being of the adoptee himself.

INDEX